LEADERS OF OUR TIME

by
Robert N. Webb

World leaders rise to power and fall; their deeds have impact upon their own nation and others, and will live after them. The twelve men in this book include not only the leaders of the four largest and strongest countries of the globe, but also leaders who rule countries of lesser size and strength. Yet each leader played a cardinal role in charting the course we are taking in the twentieth century. Some of the men in smaller countries have made as resounding an impact on global affairs as de Gaulle or Kennedy. History books have not yet been written about many of these statesmen, so these capsule biographies are a valuable insight into the personalities, policies and actions of the leaders in a troubled world.

⚜

Classification and Dewey Decimal: Biography Collection (920)

About the Author:

ROBERT N. WEBB, as a newspaperman in New England and in New York City, has interviewed many of the people who were molding the history of the early twentieth century. He has been a reporter, an editor of periodicals in the United States and in South America, and a public relations director. In recent years he has given full time to writing books for young people. A resident of Scituate, Massachusetts, Mr. Webb is married and has two children who share his interest in the events and history of the world and our times.

LEADERS OF OUR TIME

by Robert N. Webb

1966 FIRST CADMUS EDITION
THIS SPECIAL EDITION IS PUBLISHED BY ARRANGEMENT WITH
THE PUBLISHERS OF THE REGULAR EDITION
FRANKLIN WATTS, INC., BOOK PUBLISHERS
BY
E. M. HALE AND COMPANY
EAU CLAIRE, WISCONSIN

*To the staffs of the Allen Memorial and
Peirce Memorial Libraries of Scituate,
Massachusetts, the Paul Pratt Memorial
Library of neighboring Cohasset, and the
Librarian of Hanover (Mass.) High School,
this book is dedicated, in gratitude for their
friendly patience and assistance to the
author.*

CONTENTS

LEADERS
OF OUR TIME

FOREWORD

WORLD LEADERS come and go; they rise to power, they fall from power. The degree of importance of any world leader is measured by the impact he makes on his own nation and how his actions affect the whole world.

Some world leaders rise to power through their own dynamic, often ruthless, actions. For others, the mantle of world leadership settles on them automatically as they become heads of state in their own countries.

World leaders do not necessarily have to be heads of large, powerful nations. Castro leads the small island nation of Cuba; Nkrumah is the head of Ghana, a dot on the sprawling continent of Africa. Yet both these men have a resounding impact on world affairs.

The twelve men presented in this book include the

leaders of the four largest, strongest countries in the world as well as men who rule countries of lesser size and lesser strength. Each leader, however, and his country, has played an important role in charting the course the world is taking in the twentieth century.

The deeds of these men will long live after them. Their names will be prominent in history books still unwritten. It is important to know these men, not only for their impact on the world of today but for the effect of their actions on generations to come.

KONRAD ADENAUER

THE ERA OF KONRAD ADENAUER began in 1949 and ended in 1963 with the retirement of the German *Bundeskanzler*—chancellor—at the advanced age of eighty-seven.

Called the "greatest German statesman since Bismarck" by Winston Churchill, Konrad Adenauer lifted postwar Germany from shame and shambles to a position of economic strength. He led his people out of the darkness of the greatest moral and spiritual collapse in history and into the sunlight once again. Germans, despite memories of their past, could now look the world in the face without having to lower their eyes.

Konrad Adenauer (pronounced KON-raht AH-de-NOW-er) was born January 5, 1876, in Cologne, Germany, one of four children of Konrad and Helene

3

Adenauer. As a youth he attended the St. Apostein Gymnasium (high school) in Cologne. There was not much money in the Adenauer family, and young Konrad struggled through college on scholarships and part-time jobs. Later he studied at the universities of Freiburg, Munich, and Bonn, earning a degree in law.

Like his father, Adenauer's first job was as a clerk in the law courts of Cologne, and eventually he became a member of the district attorney's staff. Entering politics, he became deputy mayor and later senior deputy mayor of his home city. In 1917 he became lord high mayor of Cologne, a position he held until 1933 when he was forced out of office by the Nazis.

During his sixteen years as mayor, Adenauer showed remarkable abilities as a civic leader. Under his direction, Cologne was changed from a slow-paced Old World city to a modern, bustling one. The city's beauty was enhanced by broad belts of green parks. An annual fair was started, and it became world famous. A university and a stadium were added to the city.

Adenauer also served in the Prussian State Council as a representative of the Catholic Center Party, and he was a member of its executive committee.

When Adolf Hitler came to power in 1933, Adenauer, definitely anti-Nazi in his political feeling, was stripped of all his positions. Indeed, from that year until the end of World War II he was to spend many years in prison. Even when he was not in prison the Nazis kept a close watch on all of his activities. Much of his time during these years was devoted to writing and gardening.

In 1945, when the war ended, Germany was ruled by the four occupation powers—the United States,

Soviet Russia, England, and France. American authorities called on Adenauer and asked him whether he
would be willing to resume the office of mayor of
Cologne. Despite his age and the delicate condition of
his health, resulting from the years in prison, Adenauer
agreed. For him, a new life began at seventy. His future
greatness as chancellor of West Germany came at an
age when most men are spending their twilight years
in retirement.

Adenauer was active in the formation of the Christian
Democratic Union (CDU), a political party licensed
by the four occupation powers. In the 1949 election of
members to the Bundestag (the lower house of the West
German parliament), the CDU won a majority of the
seats. Adenauer was among those elected, and he was
then chosen by the Bundestag as chancellor.

The CDU won elections in 1953, 1957, and 1961,
and Adenauer continued as Germany's chancellor. The
Christian Democratic Union is an interdenominational
party, one that takes the middle-of-the-road course. It
attempts to solve all problems—social, economic, and
political—by the application of the principles of Chris-
tianity. It favors social security and old-age pensions,
and it looks toward the eventual reunification of East
and West Germany.

The principles and philosophy of the CDU and its
program are almost entirely Adenauer's. His long years
spent under the totalitarian rule of a ruthless, Godless
dictatorship drove Adenauer to a studious examination
of the theories of politics. One year, while a political
refugee, he lived in a Benedictine monastery. He devoted this year to extensive study of great and funda-
mental Christian documents, including such papal

encyclicals as Leo XIII's *Rerum Novarum,* written in 1891, and Pius XI's *Quadragesimo Anno* written in 1931. These documents preached the need for social reforms to draw people away from Marxist doctrines. Adenauer became convinced that society and the laws governing it must be based on Christian principles that ensure freedom and justice.

A Roman Catholic and a leader in the Catholic Center Party before the war, Adenauer took great care to see that the Christian Democratic Union did not become a Catholic party. Over half of its members are Protestants.

Adenauer's hold on the CDU was always a firm one. The party followed his lead, and its members did what he ordered. His leadership of the German government constituted almost a one-man rule. Many have charged Konrad Adenauer with using authoritarian methods to achieve his goals. In fact, some of these charges came from within his own party. The charges cannot be denied, but the authoritarian rule of Adenauer must be distinguished from that of Bismarck, Kaiser Wilhelm, and most certainly Adolf Hitler. His authoritarian leadership was for the good of his country, not for himself alone or for the purpose of recreating a strong new Germany bent on world conquest.

It is true that Adenauer suppressed opposition within his own party. He skillfully maneuvered rivals into minor positions—and kept them there. In his dealings with the Allied High Commissioners and with the heads of foreign governments, it was always he—and he alone —who handled all negotiations. In so doing, he demonstrated his dominant, authoritarian personality. He always acted according to his belief that Germans had to be told, not asked, what to do.

While it cannot be said that Adenauer was loved in his own country, he was nevertheless respected and admired. The things he worked for were the things all Germans wanted—peace, economic recovery, and stability, and to regain world esteem. His goals were the same as his people's.

As his country's leader, one of Adenauer's greatest assets was his ability to explain his policies in simple, understandable terms. Where many Germans tend to be long-winded and given to complicated, flowery statements, Adenauer used short, direct phrases that got immediately to the point.

As for German foreign policy, Adenauer set the tone when he said, "Today, I regard myself primarily as a European and only in the second place as a German." He envisioned a United States of Europe, although he did not make this goal his primary concern.

Another goal which eluded the German chancellor was the reunification of West and East Germany. Here again, however, this had not been an overriding concern in his direction of German affairs. Actually, the reunification movement in West Germany is ever present. Members of this movement are numerous and wear an identifying badge, but it is a passive rather than an active movement. West Germans believe that eventually there will be again one Germany, but that not much can be done about it now, not with Soviet Russia in firm control of East Germany.

There has been dignity and self-discipline in Adenauer's leadership of Germany. He has not hesitated to point out past German offenses against the world. Moreover, he has been equally quick to point out the great strides Germany has made to regain the moral and political approval of the Western world. One example of this was the payment by Germany of $750,-000,000 to the Republic of Israel as a symbolic gesture of atonement for Nazi atrocities against the Jews in World War II.

Adenauer is strongly anti-Communist. He has led his country toward closer and closer ties with the Western powers, the very nations Germany twice tried to conquer. Germany is a member of the European Coal Community and the European Economic Community (Common Market), and the nation is one of the strongest powers in the North Atlantic Treaty Organization. Germany supports an army of nearly 400,000—an army which serves with troops from the United States, England, and France. Combined, they face eastward toward any possible threat from Soviet Russia.

Under Adenauer bonds of friendship have been established between Germany and her ancient enemy, France. A Franco-German treaty of friendship followed an exchange of state visits between Adenauer and Charles de Gaulle, president of France.

In thus allying West Germany so completely with the Western powers, Adenauer has been hailed as a great statesman. The alliance has changed Germany's historical political pattern of playing off Eastern against Western powers, with Germany reaping the benefit. There are those in West Germany who believe better relations should be established with Russia, that the alliance with the West should be loosened. But Konrad Adenauer is strongly outspoken against such a move. There seems to be little likelihood that this movement will grow in strength unless Russia softens its attitude toward Germany. Whether or not Adenauer's successors will work toward such an accommodation with Russia will have to be seen in the future.

There can be no doubt that West Germany's reestablishment of harmonious relations with the Western powers is one of the most outstanding achievements of the Adenauer era. Paralleling this achievement, and equally significant, was West Germany's economic rise during Adenauer's fourteen years of leadership.

At the end of World War II Germany was a nation in total defeat. Many of her cities lay in ruins from heavy aerial bombardment. Her factories were idle, many of them in shambles. Her people were jobless, hungry, and hopeless. It seemed impossible that Germany could ever rise again from the rubble of its ruins and the shadow of its shame. At least, it would take a miracle for Germany to make a comeback.

Adenauer supplied that miracle. Germany's recovery under Adenauer was as miraculous as France's under de Gaulle. During the 1950s, Germany's gross national product (GNP)—the total value of goods and services produced—increased at an annual rate of 10 percent. Since then, as could be expected, this sensational annual increase has dropped to a little over 3 percent. In the early 1960s the rate of increase for the GNP has settled down to a healthy 3.5 percent, forecasting a continuing bright economic future for the German nation. By comparison, the United States had a 2.5 GNP increase during the same years.

Improvement in the lot of the German worker has kept pace with the economic rise. Over 30 percent of all German workers hold two, sometimes three, jobs. TV antennas sprout from German rooftops almost as thickly as they do in America. In a four-year period—

1954–1958—the number of German millionaires (in German marks) increased from 3,610 to 8,759.

German steel production increased from 14.8 million tons in 1936 to 34.4 million tons in 1962. The mighty Krupp factory, once the greatest munitions plant in the world, now specializes in peacetime production. Its steel plants, bridges, and heavy machinery are sold the world over, but no longer does Krupp make the tools of war.

Further, Germany enjoys a most favorable trade balance. In 1961 her exports were 1.5 billion dollars over her imports. One such export is the little Volkswagen automobile, as familiar now in every American town and hamlet as it is on European streets and highways.

Much credit for Germany's economic miracle must also be given to Economics Minister Ludwig Erhard, who succeeded Adenauer as German chancellor in the fall of 1963. Erhard, however, was not Adenauer's choice as his successor. The old chancellor publicly expressed his lack of confidence in Erhard's ability or intent to follow the path which he, Adenauer, had laid out for the German people. However, members of the Bundestag felt Adenauer had ruled long enough. They believed that his advanced age—he was eighty-seven in 1963—made him no longer an effective vote-getter with the public. The CDU voted three to one to accept Erhard over Adenauer's objections.

One of the criticisms leveled at Adenauer is that he did not groom a "crown prince" or successor. A still stronger criticism of the German leader has been that he devoted insufficient time to educating the German people in the ways of democracy. It was further said that his greatest fault was that he knew how to *sway* the people, but not how to *educate* them to become good citizens.

In this post-Adenauer era, the former chancellor will be judged by the world primarily on the question of whether the Federal Republic, which owes so much to him, will develop into a real democracy or become once more the problem nation of Europe.

Regardless of which road the post-Adenauer German pursues, *Der Alte* ("the Old One"), as Adenauer is called, will be remembered for his remarkable feat in raising Germany from ruins to riches.

On the occasion of Adenauer's eighty-second birthday, *The New York Times* said of him: "Unbowed by the years and unspoiled by success as he was undaunted by adversity, he has become an almost legendary figure in his own day."

Of his own stewardship of West Germany during his fourteen-year tenure, Adenauer said: "I only hope that, when people can look beyond the fuss and scurry of these times, they will say of me that I did my duty."

DAVID BEN-GURION

*Behold, he that keepeth Israel
shall neither slumber nor sleep.*

THIS VERSE FROM Psalm 121 most fittingly describes
a modern-day David who has tirelessly devoted his
entire life to the restoration of the nation of Israel.

David Ben-Gurion, from his early boyhood, dreamed
and worked toward the day when the Jewish people
of the world would once again have a homeland. That
dream came true and the fruits of his labors reached
maturity when, on May 14, 1948, Ben-Gurion himself
read in Hebrew the proclamation that transformed the
Jews of Palestine from a stateless people to a people with
a country they could at last call their own.

As Ben-Gurion slowly read the words that proclaimed the new Republic of Israel to a breathless crowd,
the flag of Israel, blue and white with the Star of David,

13

symbol on King David's shield, waved overhead.

The ancient nation of Israel had become reborn.

It was David Ben-Gurion who became Israel's first premier and served in that office for all but two years of the first fifteen years of the new nation's existence. In 1963, at the age of seventy-six, he retired after more than half a century of dedication to Zionism—the Jewish drive to restore the nation of Israel. In retirement he still worked to strengthen Israel, and to the world he remains "Mr. Israel."

The growth of Israel has been truly amazing. In total area, the nation is about the size of Massachusetts. Israel's Jewish population in 1948—the year the republic was proclaimed—was 600,000. In one year this population leaped to 950,000 as Jewish immigrants poured in from all over the world. When the nation celebrated its thirteenth birthday, the traditional *bar mitzvah* year when a Jewish youth attains manhood, the new republic boasted a population of over 2,100,000 and was still growing fast.

"B.G.," as Ben-Gurion is affectionately known throughout all Israel, was born David Green on October 16, 1886 in Plonsk, Poland, then a part of Russia. By the Hebrew calendar, his birth date is the 17th of Tishri in the year 5647. The Hebrew calendar is based on the date the Jews assume the earth was created.

The change in his name came when young David moved to Palestine. He wanted a name with a Biblical ring to it. Ben-Gurion resembles the names of two Jewish patriots who fought against the Romans—Bar Giora and Ben Gorion—in the last Jewish revolt in the year A.D. 135. "Gurion" in Hebrew means lion cub; "Ben" means "son of." And indeed, David Ben-Gurion was to need all the fighting strength indicated by his new name in his long struggle to bring about the rebirth of Israel.

From his earliest days, Ben-Gurion was surrounded by intellectual Jews who were dedicated to Zionism. His grandfather, Zvi Arieh, was a pioneer in the Enlightenment movement called Haskalah, aimed at reviving Hebrew as a modern language. David's father, Avigdor Green, and other Jewish community leaders in Plonsk who were members of the Lovers of Zion, gathered frequently in the Green home to read reports and discuss developments in Palestine. At this time there were two pioneer Jewish groups in Palestine. One was a small band of farmers in Galilee; the other, a colony called Petah Tiqva (Gate of Hope) formed by a band of Jews who had gone to Palestine in the first *aliyah* of modern times. Meaning literally a "going up," an *aliyah* describes a migration to Palestine.

As strongly influenced as he was by his father and his father's friends, Ben-Gurion became even more dedicated to Zionism when he read a book by one of the first great Zionist leaders, Theodor Herzl. Herzl, shocked by the growth of anti-Semitism in Europe, wrote a book called *The Jewish State*. In it he said that the only cure for anti-Semitism was mass migration of Jews to Palestine.

"The aim of Zionism," Herzl wrote, "is to create for the Jewish people a publicly recognized and legally secured home in Palestine."

Herzl formed the World Zionist Organization in 1897 in Basle, Switzerland, with Jewish representatives from countries all over the world. At that time he declared, "What glory awaits the selfless fighter for the cause! Therefore I believe that a wondrous breed of Jews will spring up from the earth . . . The Jews who will it, shall achieve their state. We shall live at last as free men on our own soil."

Inspired by these words, David Green at the age of fourteen started working actively toward Herzl's aim. From that time on, David became the "selfless fighter"; his goal, a Jewish state in Palestine.

David and two friends formed a youth group to spread the Hebrew language, to discuss the life and aims of Herzl, and to raise money to further the great cause. They called their small band the Ezra Youth Society, named after Ezra the Scribe, who had built the Second Temple in Jerusalem in Biblical times.

During the next five years, David Ben-Gurion spoke at many Zionist meetings. He went to Warsaw to study and was once thrown into jail there for his efforts to end the persecution of Jews on the college campus. Luckily, his father succeeded in getting him released.

As the 19th century ended, the persecution of Jews, particularly in eastern Europe, was mounting. In Russia the barbarous treatment of Jews caused thousands to flee to America and western Europe. In April, 1903, Jewish men, women, and children were slaughtered in a bloody pogrom at Kishinev, the capital of Russian Moldavia. A year later, Herzl died. These two tragic events caused Ben-Gurion to reach a decision which was to shape his whole future life. He felt that the only hope for the Jews was to put into action the words of Herzl and other Zionist leaders. He would move to Palestine, which was then under Turkish rule.

Since the year 1904 and continuing through 1914, a second *aliyah* of pioneers had been moving to Palestine;

their purpose was to rebuild the Holy Land. In 1906, David became a part of this historic *aliyah* which saw 40,000 Jews migrate to Palestine from Russia, Lithuania, and Poland. Nineteen-year-old Ben-Gurion felt uplifted, reborn, when the harbor of Jaffa came into view. He felt he had made the first big step toward freedom, and he wrote of this moment:

> We had left behind our books and our theorizing, the hair-splitting and the argument, and come to the Land to redeem it by our labor. We were all still fresh; the dew of dreams was moist yet in our hearts; the blows of reality had still to sober our exalted spirit.

As matters turned out, the blows came quickly, shockingly, and from an unbelievable source.

David and his friends left the port of Jaffa behind them and made a two-hour hike inland to the settlement of Petah Tiqva, founded by the men of the first *aliyah*. To David's dismay, he found that the fields and vineyards of Petah Tiqva were not being worked by the men of the first *aliyah*. These men had hired cheap Arab labor. They had become Jewish *effendis*, the Turkish name for wealthy landowners or rulers. They had long since forgotten and abandoned their original purpose for coming to Palestine—the rebuilding in Palestine of a homeland for Jews.

Ben-Gurion and his friends were refused jobs. The older, well-established group was suspicious of these young, intellectual Jews and their ideals, their dedication to the proposition that a homeland for Jews should be built by Jews working with their own hands. Even

housing and medical care were denied the young ideal-
ists. Ben-Gurion had to move on. A three-day walk
took him and his friends to Sejera. "There," David
wrote, "I found the Land of Israel."

Sejera was made up of a few dozen crude shelters.
The land had been divided into fifteen-acre plots by
the pioneer settlers. There everyone worked. Men and
women plowed the fields, weeded the gardens. Children
herded geese and milked the cows. This was the Israel
of Ben-Gurion's dreams and hopes. Here, Jewish people
were working to rebuild their original homeland.

But they did not work in peace. Hostile Arab tribes-
men often attacked the settlement. Sejera's guards were
hired Russians, outsiders, non-Jews. Ben-Gurion did
not think this right. Jews themselves should be the
guards. The elders in the village did not agree, but Ben-
Gurion carried his point, marking the beginning of his
organizational genius and leadership. A *shomer* was
formed—a defense group made up solely of Jews. The
movement spread to the villages and Ha-Shomer came
into being, Israel's first self-defense corps of Jews, the
forerunner of the Israeli defense forces which years
later were to save the new nation from destruction.

David spent two happy years in Sejera and was planning to take part in a new communal settlement experiment called a *kibbutz* when he was called to Jerusalem
by the Workers of Zion. His organizational talents, his
writing ability, and his persuasive voice were needed if
Zionism was to move forward. Ben-Gurion's immediate
job was to be a coeditor of a new Hebrew monthly
publication called *Unity*. It was 1910, and he was now
twenty-four years old. He became a full-time party
worker. The aims of the Zionist movement were to get
Turkish authorities to allow greater immigration and

to give the Jews some degree of self-government.

At first the Turkish authorities paid little attention either to *Unity* and Ben-Gurion or to the Zionist movement. The Jews were a small minority, and the idea that they wanted to be free citizens, with Hebrew recognized as an official language, seemed just a wild dream to the Turks.

To be in a better position to press the claims of Zionism, Ben-Gurion felt he should know the Turkish language and Turkish law. He already spoke Hebrew, Yiddish, and Russian. He went to Constantinople (now Istanbul) to study law so that he could "outwit the *pashas* and the *effendis*."

A year later, just as he returned to Jerusalem for a vacation, World War I broke out. It appeared that the Zionist experiment would fail just when it was beginning to move. Turkey threw in its lot with Germany. Then its government immediately ordered the expulsion of all foreign-born Jews. Ben-Gurion fought this edict, but it was a losing fight. Jews were fleeing Palestine by the thousands. Ben-Gurion and Ben-Zvi, the other editor of *Unity*, were arrested and accused of being anti-Turkish because they were trying to establish a Jewish state in Palestine. They were expelled from Turkey with the order that they were "never again to set foot on Palestine soil."

Ben-Gurion and Ben-Zvi made their way to America. Both men toured the United States and Canada, lecturing to Jewish and non-Jewish groups to arouse interest in Zionism.

During his stay in America, Ben-Gurion met and married Pauline Munwess, an immigrant from Minsk, Russia.

As Ben-Gurion and Ben-Zvi worked day and night

in America to keep their cause alive, an event took place in England that raised the hopes of Zionism the world over.

Living in England at this time was another Zionist leader, Chaim Weizmann, a scientist whose inventions in the munitions industry were helping Great Britain fight the war. Weizmann had gone to Britain from Motel, Poland, a small town not far from Plonsk, Ben-Gurion's birthplace.

Weizmann was asked by Lloyd George, secretary of state for war, how England could reward him for his contributions to the war effort. His reply was: "I would like you to do something for my people."

The Balfour Declaration, which laid the foundation for a future Jewish state was the result:

> His Majesty's Government views with favor the establishment in Palestine of a National Home for the Jewish people, and will use their best endeavors to facilitate the achievement of this object.

Jews everywhere cheered the Declaration with joy in their hearts. It seemed to them a major step toward the fulfillment of Biblical prophecies.

Ben-Gurion was spurred to even greater efforts. He also believed that the Declaration meant that Great Britain intended to extend its influence into the Middle East at the end of the war. He saw the necessity for having a trained Zionist force in Palestine when Britain began its move. He helped raise a Jewish Legion, which was sent to Palestine to serve under Field Marshal Edmund Allenby, commander-in-chief of the Egyptian

Expeditionary Force. Ben-Gurion was a member of the Jewish Legion, serving as a corporal in the Forty-second Battalion of the Royal Fusiliers.

At the war's end, Great Britain, as Ben-Gurion had foreseen, was given a mandate over Palestine. Turkish rule in Palestine thus came to an end after four hundred years.

The British mandate, approved by the League of Nations, recognized the Jewish people's right to be in Palestine. It further provided for Jewish immigration and settlement of Jews in the Holy Land.

Ben-Gurion, elated by this trend of events, hurried to Jerusalem. Later he sent for his wife, Pauline, and their infant daughter, Geula, whom he had never seen.

The years between World War I and World War II saw Ben-Gurion become the political and labor leader of the Jews in Palestine. With the help of his close friend and associate, Berl Katznelson, Ben-Gurion unified the labor movement among his people, forming the Histadrut, a Hebrew word meaning "General Federation of Labor."

Yet these were also difficult years. Arab *effendis* grew fearful of Ben-Gurion and of the increase in power of the Histadrut. There were several pogroms in the mid-1920s. Many Jews were killed and many more injured in Jerusalem. Arab hostility toward the Jews continued to increase. Moreover, a rift developed within the ranks of Zionism itself. Some felt that Ben-Gurion was trying to move too fast. Other Zionists opposed the socialist-labor tactics for rebuilding a Jewish homeland. Great Britain violated certain provisions of its mandate by curtailing immigration and limiting the sale of land in Palestine to Jews.

Despite these and many more problems, Ben-Gurion emerged as the unquestioned leader of Zionism by 1935. He was named chairman of the Jewish Executive Agency, becoming the chief spokesman for the World Zionist Organization. This marked the first time that a Palestinian Jew had been in control of all activities—worldwide—for building a Jewish homeland.

Jewish Palestine, a dagger-shaped splinter, was surrounded by enemies—Egypt, Saudi Arabia, Jordan, Lebanon, and Syria. Ben-Gurion felt that security against hostile Arabs was of foremost importance. Under the British mandate, the Jews were not permitted to maintain any defense force, but the constant raids and disorders by the Arabs forced Ben-Gurion to build one. Thus, Haganah was created (*Haganah* is the Hebrew word for defense). It became the military branch of the Jewish Executive Agency, and the British finally accepted it. Haganah, which supplied over 30,000 soldiers to the British Army during World War II, was later to play a vital part in the defense of the Republic of Israel.

While Ben-Gurion struggled with ever-increasing problems in Palestine, an even greater threat to the Jews was arising in Europe. The threat was Adolf Hitler. There were 7,500,000 Jews in Europe. Hitler's announced intention was the total elimination of all Jews.

There was no place for them to go. Immigration quotas had been set up by the United States. All European nations had their own internal problems. The only hope for the Jews was Palestine. But this hope was shattered when Great Britain in 1939 issued a White Paper limiting migration of Jews to Palestine to 15,000 a year for five years. By 1944, the British stated, all migration was to end unless the Arabs agreed to allow immigration.

Great Britain, it seemed, had turned out to be a false friend. Faced with a war with Germany, the English were wooing the Arabs but sacrificing the Jews. Winston Churchill was outspoken against the White Paper. *The New York Times* stated editorially that the British formula meant the end of the Zionist dream.

But Ben-Gurion fought on. He refused to accept the view that Zionism was ended. He would battle Britain as he battled the Arabs. But he would fight with Great Britain against Germany. "We shall fight the war as if there were no White Paper," he declared, "but we shall fight the White Paper as if there were no war."

Thousands of Palestinian Jews enlisted in the British Army. They fought on all fronts—Europe, the Middle East, and Africa.

During the war years, Ben-Gurion shuttled back and forth between England and the United States, fighting the White Paper at the same time that he and his people were fighting alongside Great Britain against the Axis powers. He constantly pounded out one idea wherever he was—the establishment of a Jewish state in Palestine.

At the end of the war, Europe was a vast graveyard of Jews. There had been 7,500,000 Jews in Europe before the war. Six million had been killed by Hitler. Of the remaining, about half made their way back to their native countries, and the others were living in displaced persons (DP) camps.

Ben-Gurion visited these camps. He saw Dachau and Belsen, where thousands of Jews had been gassed or burned alive. He returned from these visits bringing "two prayers. One, for the unity of Israel. The second, for a Jewish State, a call that goes out from the dead millions to surviving Jewry and the conscience of the world."

Ben-Gurion devoted his every energy toward having the displaced persons moved from camps and sent to Palestine. Great Britain, however, now used the White Paper as if it were the mandate. The British fleet blockaded the Palestine coast, preventing small boats from entering the port of Haifa. The ships carrying Jewish DPs were escorted to the island of Cyprus, and their human cargo was herded into barbed-wire detention camps.

Jewish terrorists struck back at the British, with the result that leaders of the Jewish Agency were arrested with two thousand other Jews. All were released without trial five months later. Ben-Gurion escaped arrest by being in Paris at the time. The British placed Palestine under martial law, sending 200,000 troops to Palestine to keep order.

Ben-Gurion renewed his shuffling between Europe and the United States. Everywhere he enlisted public and financial support. He felt certain that the end of the British mandate in Palestine was near.

Returning to Palestine in 1947, Ben-Gurion found the British, Arabs, and Jews in constant struggle. There seemed to be no solution. In England, Britain's great wartime prime minister, Winston Churchill, now leader of the opposition to the government, recommended giving up the mandate. That same year, Britain's Labour government admitted to the United Nations that its mandate was no longer workable.

In the United Nations General Assembly a Special Committee on Palestine (UNSCOP) was formed, and its first recommendation was for Great Britain to abandon its rule in Palestine, which was to become an independent country as soon as possible. On November 29, 1947, by a vote of 33 to 13, the General Assembly's decision was to partition Palestine; one area would be given to the Jews, the other to the Palestine Arabs. It was indeed a historic decision.

Six months later, at midnight of May 14, 1948, the British mandate over Palestine ended and the Republic of Israel was proclaimed. Thus, after thirty years, British rule came to a close.

Swift recognition of the new republic came from the United States. Eleven minutes after the stroke of midnight, President Harry S. Truman made the formal announcement of United States recognition. This was a tremendous morale boost to the newborn state, for it needed all the support it could get.

On the same night on which the mandate ended, the Arab Goliath attacked David's Israel. The new nation was but minutes old when it was at war. Tel Aviv was bombed three times during that same night. Five Arab armies attacked at the same time—the Egyptian Army from the south, the Syrians and Lebanese from the north, and Jordan and Iraq from the east.

Battle after battle followed. Truce followed truce as the United Nations tried to bring an end to the fighting.

Despite the war in Israel, Jews from DP camps, from Cyprus, and from Arab states flocked to their new homeland. One of Ben-Gurion's first acts had been to put into effect the Law of Return—the right of any Jew to settle in the new homeland.

Although the forces opposing Israel were overwhelming, Haganah proved its worth time and time again.

Sixty-one days after the war had begun, it was over, and Israel, under its first leader, David Ben-Gurion, was victorious. In January, 1949, the Arabs agreed to discuss armistice terms.

For the next few years an uneasy peace settled over the new republic. The principal problems now became those of building the economy and settling thousands of Jews who poured into the country faster than it could assimilate them. The capital of the republic was moved from Tel Aviv to the Jewish section of Jerusalem. The republic thrived and grew. However, the Arab threat continued to cast its shadow, and although Ben-Gurion firmly believed that the day would come when Jew and Arab would work and live together in friendship, he admitted that such a day was in the distant future.

In 1953, with the Jewish homeland in relative peace, Ben-Gurion resigned as Israel's premier to go back to the soil. For fourteen months he lived in the Kibbutz of Sdeh Boker. There he worked with his hands, toiling along with other farmers. He wanted to get away from all government activity, but this he found impossible. Hardly a day went by that he was not visited by officials from Jerusalem, seeking his advice and guidance.

Ben-Gurion was called out of retirement in 1955 to return to the Israeli cabinet as minister of defense. A few weeks later he again assumed the leadership of Israel as premier.

Before his retirement, Ben-Gurion visited America and launched Israel's first Independence Bond Issue, seeking to raise one billion dollars. The Israeli leader became a familiar figure to Americans. His squat, powerful body and his round head with its halo of white, spiky hair were seen in every major city in the United States.

But further Arab trouble was building up. In October, 1956, Gamal Abdel Nasser, president of Egypt, created a unified military command with Jordan and Syria. Its announced purpose was to "tighten the death noose" around Israel.

Israel surprised and shocked the world by taking the offensive and breaking out of this noose. Ben-Gurion ordered Israel's army to attack in the Sinai Desert and the Gaza strip to drive the Egyptians back.

The war was short. Ben-Gurion's daring and surprise attack carried the day. Although Ben-Gurion was severely criticized for launching an offensive war, he firmly believed it was the only way Israel could survive. And survive it did. The United Nations stepped in, hostilities came to an end, Ben-Gurion withdrew his army from Sinai and the Gaza strip, and UNEF—United Nations Emergency Force—took over the patrol of the Gaza strip.

The struggle by Israel for survival is far from over. But it had managed to survive against overwhelming odds when Ben-Gurion retired in 1963, on the reborn nation's fifteenth birthday. Whatever Israel's eventual fate, Ben-Gurion will long be remembered as a 20th-century Moses who led his people back to a homeland of their own.

FIDEL
CASTRO

COMMUNISM LEAPED ACROSS the Atlantic Ocean in the early 1960s to an island nation ninety miles off the coast of Florida, adding that nation to the Russian-dominated bloc of countries.

The island nation is Cuba. The man who permitted, even encouraged Communism to establish its first stronghold in the Western Hemisphere is Fidel Castro, Cuba's revolutionary leader.

"Condemn me," he challenges. "It does not matter. History will absolve me."

Will it? Will history vindicate a man who in the fourth year of his rule—1962—brought the world closer to a thermonuclear war than it had been at any time since the end of World War II? Will history pardon a man who promised his people free elections, free speech, free press, and land for all peasants, then shrugged off those promises as if he had never made them?

If Castro is to be judged solely on the events which have taken place in Cuba since January 1, 1959, the year in which he came to power, then many will condemn him. His statement that history will absolve him can be challenged if, again, the headlines of recent years are examined.

Castro made those headlines. He exploded on the world scene with all the noise and brilliance and speed of a fireworks display. In the span of a few days, the eyes of the world were focused on Cuba, the Pearl of the Antilles.

The flamboyant Castro and his small band of rebels had launched their drive to power three years before, in 1956. But reports trickling out of the Sierra Maestra, Castro's hideout and mountain fortress, had been sparse and infrequent. Only a handful of observers believed that Castro had any chance of overthrowing the iron-fisted dictator, Fulgencio Batista, and his strongly entrenched military rule. But triumph Castro did. Overnight, it seemed, Cuba had a new government.

Fidel Castro was not a penniless, hungry *peon*, as poor people are called in Spanish. Rather, his family was wealthy, and his father was a prosperous sugar planter. Fidel was born on August 13, 1927, on his family's estate in Mayari, Oriente Province. Young Castro began his education at Jesuit institutions, first at the Colegio Dolores in Santiago de Cuba, then at the Colegio Belen in Havana, where he received his bachelor's degree in 1945 at the age of eighteen. He entered the University of Havana to study law, but two years later in 1947, he interrupted his studies to become initiated into a revolutionary movement. He joined a small, ill-fated expedition against the dictatorship of the Dominican Republic. Hardly had the boat carrying Castro left the Cuban shore when it was fired upon by patrol boats. Castro leaped overboard, swam to shore, and went back to the University of Havana.

At the university he studied civil law, public administration, social sciences, and diplomacy. His undeniable qualities of leadership began showing up during his college years. Castro was a good athlete and became president of the University Students' Federation. Even then he was strongly critical of the existing government, and in one demonstration against it, he received a head injury in a fight with the police. Moreover Castro, as a wealthy student, was most generous. He helped out many other students with loans to pay for their living expenses. He finished his formal education in 1950, receiving two degrees, one of which was a doctorate in law.

Practicing law in Havana, Dr. Castro quickly gained a measure of fame by defending the poor and downtrodden, often refusing to accept any fee for his services. He was successful, too. In one case he sued and forced a landlord to reduce rents. The landlord had bribed a building inspector to condemn his tenements so that he could dispossess his tenants. Once they were ousted, the landlord readmitted them to the same tenements at double the former rent. In another case, Castro sued the government on behalf of five hundred small farm owners. A government land agency had appropriated the farms but paid their owners only half the money set aside for the appropriation, pocketing the other half.

Castro's suit forced the government to pay up in full.

In the general elections of 1952, Castro entered Cuban politics as a candidate for Parliament. That same year Batista, who had ruled Cuba since 1933 save for a period in the mid-1940s, staged a *coup d'état,* set up a harsh military dictatorship, and suspended elections.

The following year, Castro and his brother Raúl gathered a following of young men and led attacks on Batista's military establishments in the cities of Santiago de Cuba, Bayamo, and Siboney, expecting to provoke a general uprising in Oriente Province. The attacks were thrown back. Most of the rebels were killed, and Fidel and his brother were captured and imprisoned.

Fidel acted as defense attorney for himself and his brother Raúl, delivering a four-hour speech against tyranny. The speech failed to move the Batista-dictated military court—as was to be expected—and Fidel and his brother were sentenced to prison on the Isle of Pines for fifteen years. Two years later, in 1955, the brothers were released when Batista granted freedom to all political prisoners. It was a gesture he was to regret bitterly during the following years. Castro and other freed political prisoners fled to Mexico, where Castro trained the exiles in mountain warfare and guerrilla fighting against the day when he would return to Cuba. He spent one month in a Mexican jail for his activities.

In December of 1956, Castro and eighty of his followers returned to Cuba in a leaky yacht that barely made the trip. As the boat's keel ground upon the beach in Cuba, the rebels were met with gunfire from the shore. Many were killed. The survivors fled to the Sierra Maestra Mountains, densely overgrown and practically impregnable against attack. In this mountain fortress, Castro, his brother Raúl, and some fifty rebels launched the drive which was to end three years later with the overthrow of Batista. The drive was called the "26th of July Movement" in honor of their comrades who had been killed in the 1953 raids in Oriente Province.

Month by month, Castro's forces grew, although his "army" never numbered more than a thousand men during these years in the mountains. They lived and operated under the worst conditions. There was little money, little food; their weapons were of the poorest quality. There were daily skirmishes between the rebels and the government troops, with Castro always in the front line. Guerrilla raids took place, in which Castro's men raced down the mountainsides, set fire to sugar cane fields, and set off explosions in government buildings. The July 26th Movement grew as people throughout all Cuba looked to the mountains to Castro, the man who had said: "Our first fight is for political rights and after that for social rights."

The bearded Castro, clad in khaki fatigues and a long-visored cap, a rifle with telescopic sight always ready in his hands, became a symbol for Cuba. The revolutionary movement continued to grow under Castro's striking leadership and electrifying personality. Unrest stirred all over the island. Batista's days were numbered.

They came to an end on January 1, 1959, when Batista, his family, and close associates slipped out of Havana under the cover of darkness to Camp Columbia Airfield outside Havana and took flight from the island Batista had ruled so long.

One week later, on January 8, 1959, Castro rode triumphantly into Havana to the roaring cheers of thousands, hailed as Cuba's savior, idolized by his people.

But not only in Cuba was Castro hailed as the man who had driven out an iron-fisted, ruthless, brutal dictator and lifted the yoke of oppression from the necks of the Cuban people. In the United States, too, newspapers praised Cuba's new leader. He was sought after by radio and television newsmen and personalities. His bearded face became a familiar sight on American television screens.

One week after his triumphant arrival in Havana, Herbert L. Matthews wrote in *The New York Times*:

> Whatever one wants to think, everybody here seems agreed that Dr. Castro is one of the most extraordinary figures ever to appear on the Latin American scene. He is by any standards a man of destiny.

In April, four months after his victory, Castro came to the United States at the invitation of the American Society of Newspaper Editors. He received an openhanded welcome. Castro's striking personality, his eagerness to please, brought him cheering, favorable receptions wherever he went.

A few weeks later, this popular picture of Castro changed. Indeed, it was completely reversed. No other man in modern history has publicly made such a complete about-face in such a short period of time as Fidel Castro. Overnight, the real Castro replaced the public image of the hero and savior, and his doctrine of "hate Yankeeism" boiled to the surface.

As the picture changed, more of Castro's characteristics were revealed. A few days after his entry into

Havana, he stated: "I promise to solve every problem without bloodshed. I promise Cuban mothers no more shots will be fired." But even as these words were being cheered in Cuba and the author of them was visiting in the United States, the executions of over 550 "war criminals" were being carried out.

Other steps were taken by Castro which were in exact contradiction to his announced idealistic motives for the revolution. There would be no free elections. A tight muzzle of censorship was clamped on the press; newspapers opposing Castro and his methods were seized. Social and civil rights promised by Castro were forgotten. Farmlands and cattle were seized. Peasant tenant farmers, who were granted the minimum sixty-six acres promised, found those acres had to be worked as government cooperatives.

Castro was quickly adopting many of the procedures of Communist rule. Seizure of property without payment became the rule. All large and many small businesses were taken over.

United States interests had very large investments in Cuba. Among others, these included about 40 percent of its sugar production, 80 percent of its utilities, 90 percent of its mines, and all of its oil refineries.

At the same time, the United States was Cuba's largest customer and took a large part of its sugar crop at guaranteed prices, as well as a large part of its tobacco crop. In addition, Cuba was a favorite vacation place for Americans.

A Communist state next door to the United States caused great alarm, both in the United States and through Latin America. Cubans who were associated with foreign businesses began to flee the country, often with no more than the clothes on their backs; soon they were followed by thousands more.

Castro encouraged such slogans as "Yankee go home!" and "Cuba si! Yankee no!" He and his followers made long speeches blaming all their troubles and problems on "Yankee Imperialism." As so often in history, a man who has the power to sway the masses is a leader.

Nevertheless, many reports came through the press stating that Castro was a chronic drunk, that he never kept appointments, and that his days of rule would be short, for he would be shot either by an enemy or by an associate. How much of this was true few could tell; the point was that he kept going ahead, establishing a Communist state right next to the United States of America.

The United States hoped that Castro would take a reasonable stand and work out some basis upon which the two countries could work together in harmony. So far, at least, the bearded leader had not declared himself to be a Communist.

Then Castro suddenly began to confiscate American holdings in Cuba. In retaliation the U.S. cut off Cuba's sugar quota, whereby that country had a large share of the American market at a guaranteed price, set above the world price.

Castro's next step was to order the United States to reduce the number of diplomatic representatives in Cuba. Finally, on January 3, 1961, just two years after Castro had assumed power, the United States broke off diplomatic relations with the island nation.

Many people felt that the United States should dispose of Castro by using armed force if necessary, but the United States government was determined to stand by the policy of not intervening in the governments of Latin America. There were meetings of the Organization of American States in which resolutions denouncing Castro were passed by a majority, but the larger countries—Brazil, Mexico, and Argentina—did not vote.

Since there was no sentiment at all in Latin America for a joint armed intervention, the United States did not press the matter.

Castro obviously guessed the sentiment right. While his own government was not friendly with any of the other governments, none of the latter felt that they wanted to risk joining in a war against him. Moreover, while most Latin American countries join with the United States in the United Nations on many matters affecting the world, and are genuinely friendly to the United States, they nevertheless resent the thought of Yankee interference with the internal affairs of Cuba.

Many exiles from Cuba in the United States wanted to form an army of liberation. They believed that a small force would be welcomed by the Cuban people and that parts, if not all of the army would revolt. In April of 1961 a force of 1,500 young Cubans invaded their homeland at the Bay of Pigs. The invasion failed. Many were killed, and some 1,100 were captured and thrown into prison. Castro hailed this victory as a triumph over the United States, although Uncle Sam actually took no official part in the invasion.

After twenty months in prison, the prisoners were freed by Castro for a ransom of $53,000,000 in food and medicines sent from the United States.

A crisis of world proportions was brought on by Castro in the fall of 1962, revealing that Cuba had indeed become a full-fledged Russian satellite. At that time

United States Air Force reconnaissance planes, flying low sweeps over Cuba, photographed the installation of Russian missiles and launching pads. Alarm was understandably great, for these were "offensive" weapons capable of delivering nuclear warheads to any city in the United States. Acting immediately, President Kennedy delivered an ultimatum to Soviet Russia's Premier Khrushchev demanding that these missiles be dismantled and the Russian military personnel manning them be removed. The whole world waited in breathless fear. Was this the spark that would touch off a thermonuclear war? But Premier Khrushchev backed down. He agreed to the terms of President Kennedy's ultimatum and a sigh of relief swept the world. The missiles were removed. Yet Soviet Russia still maintains a military establishment in Cuba, the size of which is a matter of widely differing opinions.

Castro and Cuba, of course, cannot be disassociated. But a line can be drawn between the actions of Castro the man and the actions of the Cuban people in following him. It cannot be said that Castro is a product of those very conditions in Cuba—which he promised to change and has not—that created the Cuban's hatred of the United States. On the contrary, Castro came from a family that was a member of Cuba's wealthy, ruling class.

A self-centered man who inspires loyalty but does not give it, Castro is first, last, and always for Castro. An aide and close friend of Castro's who saved his life during the 1953 raids in Oriente is now serving a twenty-year prison sentence at Castro's orders.

But it can be said of Castro that he is a spectacular leader of men with a magnetic personality that overwhelms his followers. A striking figure of a man, he is six feet tall and powerfully built. He affects a scraggly beard, has brown eyes and curly brown hair, and wears horn-rimmed glasses. Seldom is he seen without a Havana cigar jutting out of his strong, firm mouth. Although he considers himself a devout Roman Catholic, he was married and later divorced. He has one son.

Following Russia's withdrawal of its missiles from Cuba, Castro's prestige dipped, but not sufficiently for him to lose any control over his police state. In the spring of 1963, six months after the missile withdrawal, Castro went to Russia, where he received a state reception that outdid any given by the Soviet Union to any other visiting dignitary or head of state. Any breach between Castro and Premier Khrushchev caused by the missile withdrawal was closed by this state visit, and Cuba remained as close an ally of Russia as ever.

The question as to whether Castro himself is a Communist is often raised. Students of Castro's career do not believe him to be a Communist, although he has openly declared his belief in the teachings of Lenin. Nor is he a mere puppet of Moscow, dancing a jig when Russia pulls the strings. On the other hand, Castro's brother Raúl, who commands the Cuban military, is believed to be a dedicated Communist.

The Cuban chief of state is a man of many contradictions. If he were not so dependent on Russia, he could break with the Soviet as quickly as he previously joined with it. But, whatever one may think of him, it would be foolish to blind oneself to the fact that Castro is a serious threat to the Western Hemisphere.

How history will judge this man only time can tell. There can be no doubt, however, that he has made his mark in the world, and that mark is Red.

CHARLES
DE GAULLE

THE RESTORATION OF FRANCE to its former grandeur is the driving force behind a tall, impressive Frenchman who has devoted his entire life to his beloved country. In recent years, he has pulled France back from the brink of becoming a second-rate power to a position of dominance in Europe, making it a nation to be reckoned with in world-wide power politics.

This aloof, austere, slow-spoken Frenchman is Charles de Gaulle (pronounced de GOAL), President of the French Republic and the French Community since 1959. Under his leadership France made a spectacular economic and fiscal comeback from the edge of bankruptcy. Indeed, within five years of de Gaulle's ascendancy to power, France became a healthy, wealthy nation, its industries humming, its economic growth on the rise, its monetary unit, the franc, firm and strong after years of being one of the shakiest of international currencies.

With its economic rise—often called the "French miracle"—the nation also regained its world-wide prestige, which had been at an extremely low ebb before de Gaulle took office. By exploding an atom bomb in the Sahara Desert in 1959 France joined the exclusive nuclear club—a club whose other members are the United States, Great Britain, and Soviet Russia.

Charles de Gaulle, who wields more personal power than any French ruler since Napoleon, has also demonstrated his strength in other areas. In 1963, for example, he prevented Great Britain from joining the Common Market of Europe. De Gaulle has been in frequent disagreement with the United States on the defense of Europe and has disowned former French commitments to the North Atlantic Treaty Organization (NATO). He withdrew the French naval force from NATO's Mediterranean fleet. He has refused to permit the location of intercontinental ballistic missiles on French soil, unless he has a voice in deciding who is to trigger them. The United States had to withdraw much of its military forces for the defense of Europe from French soil and relocate them in England and Germany because, again, de Gaulle insisted that he have a voice in how they would be used.

De Gaulle's rise to power was as rapid as his country's economic recovery. France was restored to much of its former grandeur, and during the restoration de Gaulle became *le grand Charles*, the strongest leader in western Europe.

Charles André Joseph Marie de Gaulle was born in Lille, France on November 22, 1890, the second of five children. He had three brothers and one sister. Most of his youth was spent in Paris, where his father, Henri de Gaulle, was a professor of philosophy in a Jesuit school. After completing his secondary schooling and his required military service, de Gaulle entered Saint-Cyr, a French military school which is the equivalent of the United States Military Academy at West Point. This was the beginning of de Gaulle's long, honorable, and illustrious service to his country.

De Gaulle was commissioned a second lieutenant upon graduating from Saint-Cyr and first saw service in the Thirty-third Infantary Regiment under Colonel Henri Pétain. The lives of these two men were to cross and recross in friendship and enmity in the troubled years that led to the downfall of France in World War II.

During World War I, de Gaulle proved himself to be a daring soldier. Volunteering for the most dangerous missions, he was wounded in action on three occasions, first in 1914 at Dinant, again in 1915 at Champagne, and a third time at Douaumont in 1916. The wounds he received at Douaumont were so severe that he was captured by the Germans and spent the next two years in German prison camps.

At the close of World War I, de Gaulle was repatriated with other French prisoners and continued his military service. He served with the French army in Poland, then returned to Saint-Cyr, where he taught military history.

De Gaulle was now a commandant in the French army. He had formed strong opinions about military science and strategy, opinions which ran contrary to those of his superiors. He was attending the École Supérieure de Guerre (War College) in Paris when he first demonstrated his opposition to the military tactics France had employed for years. During annual maneuvers de Gaulle used mobile tactics with his command, thus flying in the face of tradition. Military principles in France at this time were the defensive, dig-in tactics developed during the trench warfare of World War I. Because he opposed such tactics outspokenly and in practice, de Gaulle was demoted.

De Gaulle's first commanding officer, Henri Pétain, heard of the incident. Pétain had risen to commander-in-chief and marshal of the French army. He immediately reinstated de Gaulle to his rank as commandant, appointed him an instructor at the War College, and made him a member of his own staff. But twenty years later, as head of the German-controlled French government at Vichy, Pétain was to appoint the court-martial which condemned de Gaulle to death, *in absentia*, for treason. De Gaulle was then in England.

From 1927 until the outbreak of World War II, de Gaulle served in many military posts. He was on the general staff of the French Army of the Rhine as commander of the Nineteenth Battalion of the Chasseurs à Pied. He headed military missions to Egypt, Syria, Iraq, and Persia (now called Iran). Returning to France in 1932, he was named secretary-general of the High Council of National Defense, with the rank of lieutenant colonel.

Once again de Gaulle's military theories and those of the French High Command clashed. In 1934 he published a book in which he sharply criticized the French military strategy based on the Maginot Line. This Line was a series of concrete defense structures stretched across the northern border of France, which were supposed to make France impregnable against attack. De Gaulle said they would not hold back an attack, and he predicted the blitzkrieg tactics with which the Germans were later to overrun France in World War II. Although de Gaulle was correct, his ideas for a fast-striking, mobile force were not accepted by the French General Staff.

During the next five years, de Gaulle did develop a small mechanized force, placing his main reliance upon tanks. But by the time of Germany's attack, France had only three light mechanized divisions and four heavy armored divisions. These were not sufficient to turn back the Germans, who, with their heavy armor and mechanized troops, overran the Maginot Line and swept through France in May and June of 1940.

De Gaulle, as a brigadier general in command of the small French mechanized forces, held the Germans at Laon and Abbeville for a time, but the Germans were not to be denied. By June 15, 1940, it was all over. France was defeated.

Just before the final German victory, de Gaulle had been named undersecretary of national defense and war by Premier Paul Reynaud, and he had gone to London to confer with Prime Minister Winston Churchill. By the time he returned to France, on June 15, the new French premier, Marshal Pétain, had signed a truce with Germany. De Gaulle refused to acknowledge the truce, refused to admit France had been defeated, and fled to London.

In London de Gaulle formed a French National Committee which was to operate as France's government.

The group was called the Free French, and de Gaulle was made the president. The Pétain government in Vichy, France, refused to recognize de Gaulle or the government he established; they called him a traitor and tried him for treason, sentencing him to death. But de Gaulle had the backing of the British government, which recognized him as commander of the Free French Army. He also had the backing of the resistance movements which sprang up in France during the German occupation.

De Gaulle continued as head of the many Free French and resistance movements for the remainder of the war. He was made president of the Provisional Government of the French Republic in May of 1944, and from Algeria he went to London, where he awaited the Normandy invasion.

The stubborn de Gaulle, the man who refused to accept the defeat of his country, returned to Paris in triumph on August 24, 1944, with the victorious Allied armies.

In the hectic postwar years, de Gaulle was head of the provisional government of France. The nation was in the throes of drafting a constitution for the Fourth Republic and de Gaulle urged radical changes in the new constitution, proposing a strong presidency to balance the powers of the legislature. Under the constitutions of the first three French republics, the president had had little or no power. De Gaulle's proposals were not accepted, and he resigned in January, 1946. The Fourth Republic was proclaimed in October, 1946, with a constitution along traditional lines.

For the next eleven years, de Gaulle held no public office. Although in retirement, he continually called for sweeping reforms in the framework of the French government.

Again de Gaulle proved to be a prophet. After ten years, the Fourth Republic, with its weak constitution, was near bankruptcy and civil war. There had been one cabinet crisis after another. In May, 1958, President René Coty called de Gaulle out of retirement, and he served the Fourth Republic as its premier from June, 1958 to January, 1959. During these months, de Gaulle pushed hard for a new constitution, which was adopted by 78 percent of the French voters on September 28, 1958. This new constitution provided the president's office with sweeping powers and relegated the legislature to a minor position, in contrast to the constitutions of the first four French republics.

De Gaulle was elected president of the Fifth Republic for a term of seven years, taking office in January of 1959. Assured of holding office for seven years, and with a constitution he practically wrote himself, de Gaulle faced mountainous problems at home and abroad. But he had the power to deal with them.

There were, and still are, many critics of the tremendous powers held by the president of France. The legislature, under the constitution of the Fifth Republic, is a body with hardly more power than the former presidents of France previously held. Thus the balance of power has been reversed.

The swift return of France to a position of world influence was de Gaulle's answer to critics of his Napoleonic powers. There is no doubt that he holds such powers, but he has used them for France.

The formation by de Gaulle of the French Community in 1958 solved many of France's colonial problems. Twelve French African colonies became self-governing states but remained within the French Community by continuing close economic and political ties with Paris.

The long and costly Algerian war was ended in 1962. De Gaulle offered Moslem rebels a truce that would lead to Algeria's independence. French militarists in Algeria, dead set against independence for the country, conducted a reign of terror for months after the truce was offered. On July 1, 1962, however, Algeria voted for complete independence from France. De Gaulle so proclaimed it two days later.

On the home front, one of de Gaulle's most spectacular moves, and the one of which he is reportedly most proud, was his action to establish friendly relations with France's long-time enemy—Germany. Although he fought twice against Germany, de Gaulle on a state visit to that nation spoke of the German people thus: *"Das deutsche Volk ist ein grosses Volk"* —"the German people are a great people." A proposed treaty of "cooperation and friendship" with Germany was bitterly argued throughout all France. But in the end, de Gaulle's treaty became a reality. In the spring of 1963 the French National Assembly approved it by a vote of 325 to 107.

France's economic recovery remains de Gaulle's outstanding accomplishment. The nation's gross national product has increased steadily at a rate of 5.5 percent as compared to the 2.5 percent GNP growth of the United States. France tripled its gold and dollar reserves in the first four years of de Gaulle's reign. Her state-owned railroads operate on time. The Renault auto company, also state-owned, is thriving, and its tiny

Dauphines dot even American suburbs. French farmers are producing 40 percent more wheat than they did before World War II.

France's remarkable economic upsurge has been matched by that of other European countries, particularly the members of the Common Market, also known as the European Economic Community. The original members of the Common Market were France, West Germany, Italy, Luxembourg, Belgium, and the Netherlands. These countries have prospered through the elimination of many trade barriers and sharp reductions in tariff rates. In the first three years of the Common Market, trade among its members increased by 73 percent, and the Common Market members' total world trade rose by 23 percent, faster than any other country in the Western bloc. Industrial production had a comparable growth, and total product, including farming, increased by 20 percent.

Great Britain was originally invited to become a member of the Common Market, but she refused. When five years later Great Britain tried to join the group, in 1963, she was denied admittance. It was de Gaulle's veto which kept Great Britain out.

De Gaulle's distrust of Great Britain is closely linked with his opposition to the United States' influence in European affairs. De Gaulle has stated that he does not consider Great Britain to be a European country, since she is tied so closely both economically and militarily to the United States. Moreover, he firmly believes that when Great Britain has to choose between Europe and the United States on an issue, the British always side with their American ally.

De Gaulle's conflict with the United States stems

from his stated belief that the United States would not risk its cities to nuclear bombardment in the event of an attack on any of the NATO countries. For this reason he refused to commit France to full cooperation with the North Atlantic Treaty Organization. The French leader reasoned that should any NATO country be attacked by conventional forces, the United States would think twice before coming to Europe's support because its cities might thereby become subject to retaliatory attacks by long-range nuclear missiles. The United States, he felt, wanted Europe to supply the conventional ground forces as a bulwark between itself and the Communists. And this is in spite of the fact that United States armed forces in Europe are as large or larger than those of any other NATO country.

In the early summer of 1963, while President Kennedy was on a visit to Europe to strengthen the NATO alliance, he reiterated the United States' position of its full commitment to defend Europe in the event of an enemy attack.

De Gaulle at this time envisioned a Europe strong enough to defend itself without relying completely on the United States for its survival. His dream was that of strong European nations, each capable of defending itself with nuclear striking power of its own. De Gaulle, whose driving nationalism led France back to self-respect, found himself in a strange position as Europe prospered. The fierce nationalistic feelings which had marked European nations in the past were disappearing. Europe was changing. Europeans by car, bus, train, and motor scooter were traveling from one country to another as readily as a New Yorker travels to New Jersey, Connecticut, or Pennsylvania. European frontiers were disappearing. De Gaulle remained almost alone as the champion of nationalism.

The French leader's firm hold on his people has been demonstrated time and time again. He makes effective use of television to "go to the people" when opposition to any of his proposals arises. Although by nature an aloof man, he travels to the most remote villages of France to talk to his people.

Two attempts have been made upon his life, but he shrugs these off. He is the despair of his bodyguards.

Perhaps no other world leader is as imposing looking as Charles de Gaulle. He is six feet, four inches tall, has blue eyes and thinning brown hair, and his tremendous nose has been described as "elephantine." In 1921, de Gaulle married Yvonne Charlotte Anne-Marie Vendroux. They had three children: Phillippe, a naval officer; a daughter Elizabeth; and a second daughter, Anne, who died.

De Gaulle will be long remembered for his restoration of French prestige and for his dominant part in the politics and economy of a changing Europe. Despite criticism of his one-man rule, his broad powers which have made him an "elected king," this French patriot pulled his country up by its bootstraps until La Belle France stood as tall in the world's eyes as her president stands among the world's leaders.

JOHN F. KENNEDY

WHEN JOHN F. KENNEDY became the thirty-fifth president of the United States, he became not only the leader of his country but one of the leaders of the world. This second unofficial, yet highly important, position comes automatically to any man when he takes the oath of office as president of the United States.

America's role in international affairs and her leadership of the nations of the Free World is one of grave responsibility. The United States, by her own example and by her announced determination that there shall always be free peoples in the world, has become a bulwark against the spread of Communism.

These added responsibilities, therefore, fall upon the shoulders of the man who solemnly swears: "I will faithfully execute the Office of President of the United States, and will to the best of my Ability, preserve, protect and defend the Constitution of the United States."

John F. Kennedy accepted this awesome responsibility, these staggering burdens, on January 20, 1961. He was immediately confronted with problems on the home front and with problems on the international scene. World problems so directly affect domestic ones in these times that a "brush fire" in the Congo, a border dispute in Asia, a pronouncement from the Kremlin, all had to be viewed for their effect on the security and economy of the United States by Kennedy, the youngest man ever elected president. (Theodore Roosevelt was younger, actually, when he assumed the presidency after the assassination of President McKinley, but he had not been elected to the office at that time.)

While youth stepped onto the world stage when Kennedy took office, the other key figures in world leadership in 1961 were all men of advanced age. Dwight D. Eisenhower, the man Kennedy succeeded as president, was seventy-one; West Germany's leader, Konrad Adenauer, was eighty-five; Khrushchev was sixty-seven; England's Macmillan was also sixty-seven; de Gaulle of France was seventy-one; India's Nehru was seventy-two; and Red China's Mao Tse-tung was sixty-eight.

John F. Kennedy was forty-three.

The ages of these other leaders is a matter of grave concern throughout the world and of particular concern in the nations where these elder statesmen have ruled for so many years. The younger generations watch restlessly as the years settle on the tiring shoulders of these heads of state. What happens when time runs out on a

Above: West German Chancellor Konrad Adenauer addressing members of the National Press Club in Washington during his visit to the United States in 1962.

Right: "Der Alte" outlines policy in an address to the Bundestag in Bonn, February, 1963. In background is Ludwig Erhard, then economic minister, and now Adenauer's successor.

Photos by Wide World

Israeli Prime Minister David Ben-Gurion in November, 1956.   He has just arrived at Parliament in Jerusalem to hear a report on the Israeli victory in Egypt.

Above: Ben-Gurion speaking to delegates of the fifth international meeting of Biological Standardization at the Hebrew University in Jerusalem, September, 1959. Below: Ben-Gurion quells applause as he is introduced to speak at Jewish Theological Seminary in New York, March, 1960.

Premier Fidel Castro of Cuba is shown here in typical poses during one of his lengthy informal broadcasts to the Cuban people.

A face familiar the world over — President Charles de Gaulle of France.

John Fitzgerald Kennedy, thirty-fifth President of the United States.

On the way to the Capitol. Retiring President Dwight D. Eisenhower and his youthful successor, John F. Kennedy, prepare to ride to the Capitol together for Kennedy's Inauguration.

At the Capitol. John F. Kennedy is shown being sworn in as thirty-fifth President of the United States by Chief Justice Earl Warren.

Presidential news conference. Before the television cameras, in typical poses like these, President Kennedy regularly informed the nation — and the world — on vital issues.

Soviet Premier Nikita Khrushchev addresses a gathering of newsmen in Washington, D.C., during his visit to the United States in 1959. He told the newsmen: "I look upon you as my fellow travelers, my sputniks." On his right lapel, Khrushchev is wearing the Lenin Peace Medal.

Prime Minister Harold Macmillan of Britain smiles confidently after winning a vote of confidence in the House of Commons in June, 1963. Forced to resign after a serious operation, he was succeeded by Lord Home in October of the same year.

Mao Tse-tung, Leader of the Chinese Communists and Chairman of the Central People's Government of the Chinese People's Republic. Photo was taken during Mao's visit to Moscow in 1950.

President Gamal Abdel Nasser of Egypt, 1960.

Indian Prime Minister Jawaharlal Nehru strikes various poses as he addresses the United Nations General Assembly in November, 1961. On this occasion, Nehru warned world leaders that they must either end the threat of nuclear war or burrow into the earth and live like rats.

Nehru at ease. Sitting informally on a table, the Indian Prime Minister speaks at an open-air meeting in Char Duar, near the foothills in northeast India, 1962. He was visiting forward positions in the areas of the frontier battle with the Chinese Communists.

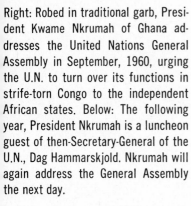

Right: Robed in traditional garb, President Kwame Nkrumah of Ghana addresses the United Nations General Assembly in September, 1960, urging the U.N. to turn over its functions in strife-torn Congo to the independent African states. Below: The following year, President Nkrumah is a luncheon guest of then-Secretary-General of the U.N., Dag Hammarskjold. Nkrumah will again address the General Assembly the next day.

U Thant of Burma at the United Nations in late 1961. Mentioned as possible United Nations Secretary-General to succeed the late Dag Hammarskjold, he was unanimously elected as Acting Secretary-General on November 3 of that year.

Mao, a Khrushchev, a Nehru, the leaders of the three most populous countries in the world? This question became more sharply pointed up when the forty-three-year-old Kennedy took his position among the leaders of the world.

John Fitzgerald Kennedy was born on May 29, 1917, in Brookline, Massachusetts, a suburb of Boston. He was the second of nine children of Joseph P. Kennedy, Sr., and Rose Fitzgerald Kennedy. Both his grandfathers were the sons of Irish immigrants who came to America after the potato famine in Ireland in 1847. Both became prominent in Massachusetts politics. Patrick J. Kennedy, a saloon-keeper, served in both houses of the Massachusetts legislature. John F. ("Honey Fitz") Fitzgerald was a mayor of Boston.

The future president grew up in an atmosphere heavily filled with political discussions, local, national, then international. His father was an ardent supporter of Franklin D. Roosevelt in the 1932 presidential campaign. In 1933 Roosevelt appointed him as chairman of the Securities and Exchange Commission, and in 1937 he became the United States Ambassador to Great Britain. Young John Kennedy served as his father's secretary in the London Embassy. His interest in England's problems at the approach of World War II resulted in his first published book, *Why England Slept*.

The Kennedys were a wealthy family. The children were reared in a spirit of family closeness and loyalty, and from their mother, a devoted Catholic, they received a deep sense of religious obligation. Their father encouraged competition among the children, and to give them all a sense of their responsibility in public life, he settled on each child one million dollars, which the children would receive upon reaching maturity.

The Kennedy family moved to a New York suburb in 1926, as Joseph Kennedy wanted his family near the Wall Street headquarters of his many financial enterprises. They spent their summers in Hyannisport on Cape Cod.

John F. Kennedy attended a Catholic school for only one year, the Canterbury School in New Milford, Connecticut. He received his secondary education at the Choate School in Wallingford, Connecticut. He entered Princeton following a summer at the London School of Economics in the fall of 1935, but left after a few months because of illness.

In 1936, Kennedy joined his older brother Joseph at Harvard, their father's alma mater. John was a member of the swimming team, and he and Joseph won the intercollegiate sailing championship. John went out for football, but his light weight was against him. During his sophomore year, he suffered a spinal injury during scrimmage that later threatened his political career and even his life. Kennedy was also a member of the editorial staff of the *Harvard Crimson*, the college daily newspaper.

The future president majored in political science at Harvard. It was his thesis on England's unpreparedness for war that he later developed into the book, *Why England Slept*. He was graduated from Harvard with a B.S. degree *cum laude* in 1940. He then went to Stanford University to study business administration and followed this with a tour of South America. On his return to this country, he tried to enlist in the Navy, undergoing extensive medical treatment before he was accepted, six months after he had filed application. He applied for active duty, but a year passed before he was assigned to a motor torpedo boat squadron in 1942.

In August of 1943, Lieutenant John F. Kennedy was in command of PT–109 on patrol off the Solomon Islands. When a Japanese destroyer torpedoed the PT–109, Kennedy was given up for lost for several weeks. But he was still alive, and he is credited with saving the lives of several crewmen. One injured crewman Kennedy heroically towed through the water for three miles to an island. The young naval officer accomplished this feat by means of a life belt held in his teeth as he swam. Kennedy insisted on remaining on active duty, but in December he was sent back to the United States, where he spent several months in a naval hospital in Massachusetts.

It was while he was recuperating from his Pacific injuries that word came of the death of his older brother, Joseph. Joseph, a Navy pilot, was shot down on a flight over the English Channel. His death, according to many Kennedy biographers, marked a turning point in the career of his younger brother, since Joseph had been considered the member of the family who would carry on the Kennedys' political heritage.

During the two years before he first ran for political office, John F. Kennedy worked as a newspaperman, covering the United Nations organization conference in San Francisco. He was a foreign correspondent in Europe for the International News Service, covering the Potsdam Conference attended by President Truman, Prime Minister Churchill, and Premier Stalin.

Kennedy became a member of the House of Representatives in 1946, winning the election in Massachusetts'

Eleventh Congressional District. He served three terms as a member of the House before deciding, in 1952, to run for the Senate. He was opposed by the Republican incumbent, Senator Henry Cabot Lodge. Kennedy, with the aid of his family, waged a strenuous, whirlwind campaign. He rang doorbells, gave tea parties, traveled all over the state. In the Republican landslide of that year which brought Eisenhower the presidency and carried Massachusetts by 200,000 votes, Kennedy won out, defeating Lodge by over 70,000 votes.

In his eight years as a senator Kennedy served on the Government Operations Committee, the Labor and Public Welfare Committee, the Foreign Relations Committee, and the Joint Economic Committee. His record in the House and in the Senate shows him to have been a moderate liberal, standing neither to the extreme left or extreme right in his party's policies. He showed this independence early, refusing when he first ran for Congress to identify himself firmly with any element of his party.

During Kennedy's second year as a senator, he was forced to undergo surgery for the spinal injuries suffered at football, which had become further aggravated during his service in the Pacific. A long period of recuperation followed, preventing him from attendance in the Senate during most of 1955. During his long, bedridden months, Kennedy wrote a series of short biographies called *Profiles in Courage.* These dealt with American legislators who had shown their courage by withstanding pressure from their constituents to stand up for what they believed was right. The book was an immediate best seller and in 1957 won the Pulitzer Prize in biography.

During his first term as senator, John F. Kennedy married Jacqueline Lee Bouvier on September 12, 1953. Mrs. Kennedy is the daughter of John V. Bouvier, a New York financier, and the stepdaughter of Hugh D. Auchincloss. Their wedding at Newport, Rhode Island, was one of the outstanding social events of the year. Mrs. Kennedy is a charming, gracious lady, twelve years younger than her husband. Her beauty, her warmth, her style, have made a strong impact both in the United States and abroad. The Kennedys have two children, a daughter Caroline and a son, John Fitzgerald, Jr. A third child was born in 1963 but died soon after birth.

National political prominence came to Kennedy during the Democratic National Convention in Chicago in August of 1956. A sudden ground swell put him in the running for the nomination for vice-president, to team with Adlai Stevenson on the Democratic ticket. But Kennedy lost out to Estes Kefauver. However, when Stevenson and Kefauver were defeated by the Eisenhower ticket, Kennedy became the Democrats' bright hope as they looked toward 1960. These hopes became even brighter when Kennedy, running for re-election to the Senate in 1958, won the office with a record-breaking 869,000 majority.

When the Democratic National Convention of July, 1960 rolled around, Kennedy was the No. 1 choice for the presidential nomination. His most formidable opposition came from Senator Lyndon B. Johnson of Texas, who later became Kennedy's vice-presidential running mate. Kennedy was nominated on the first ballot.

His opponent for the presidency was Richard M. Nixon of California, who had been Eisenhower's vice-president for eight years. In a hot, closely contested

campaign, Kennedy won out over Nixon by the slim-
mest of margins, defeating him by less than 120,000
votes. It was generally conceded that the four nationally
televised debates between the two candidates were the
vital factor which carried the day for Kennedy. Kennedy proved to be the more "telegenic" of the two, and
more importantly, through the debates Kennedy became
as well known as Nixon, a man who had been an extremely active vice-president, both nationally and inter-
nationally, under Eisenhower.

Kennedy became the first Catholic president in the
history of the United States. Although religion was not
recognized as an issue between the two candidates, Kennedy had to repeatedly affirm his belief in the separation
between church and state. A survey of the voting by the
University of Michigan drew the conclusion that the
religious issue had been important, and that Kennedy's
faith had cost him 1,500,000 votes.

Kennedy's inaugural address was hailed for its "shin-
ing rhetoric"; it is best remembered for its singing words
as he said, "Ask not what your country can do for you;
ask what you can do for your country."

Although he barely squeaked by in winning the presidency, Kennedy's increase in popularity after he became the thirty-fifth president was tremendous, rivaling
that of his predecessor. His popularity at home was
equaled by that in foreign countries. On trips to South
America and Europe, millions lined the streets to cheer
the smiling, youthful American president. This popularity has had its ups and downs, as it has with all presidents, but Kennedy during his first three years of office
remained an exceptionally popular president with the
American people.

This popular support, however, did not carry the same weight for Kennedy with the Congress as it had for Roosevelt. Congress, remembering Kennedy's narrow margin of victory, did not go along in full support of Kennedy's program. A coalition of Southern Democrats and Republicans worked to defeat several measures the president asked Congress to pass. Among them were medical care for the aged under Social Security and federal aid to education.

On the positive side, the most important legislation the president asked for—and got—was the Trade Expansion Act. Under this act the president has the authority to reduce or even eliminate tariffs so as to place the United States favorably in competition with the European Economic Community, better known as the Common Market.

The president also asked for the establishment of a Peace Corps of workers who would live and work in remote parts of the world, helping native populations through education, by imparting agricultural knowledge, and by medical attention. This request was favorably acted upon by the Congress and enthusiastically supported by the American people.

In other areas the president's foreign aid requests were supported, although the requested appropriation was sliced. Increased social benefits were approved, a new housing authority was set up, and a revised minimum wage bill was passed by the Congress.

Elsewhere on the home front, the racial integration problem took the headlines and held them month after month. In this sensitive area Ralph McGill, publisher of the progressive Atlanta *Constitution*, stated his belief that the Kennedy Administration had done more to improve the lot of the Negro in the United States than any other administration.

On the international scene, Kennedy inherited the uneasy peace from the preceding administration. Toward the end of his second year in office, Kennedy was faced with a crisis that threatened to turn into a third world war, a devastatingly destructive nuclear war. Aerial photographs showed the installation in Cuba—ninety miles off the United States mainland—of Russian offensive missiles, capable of destroying any city in the country. President Kennedy immediately ordered a "strict quarantine of all offensive military equipment under shipment to Cuba." In a television address, the president told a worried America that American naval and air forces were constantly circling the island of Cuba. He stated that this was but the first step and that further action would be taken if Russia did not immediately remove its missiles.

The nation waited breathlessly for Premier Khrushchev's reply to Kennedy's ultimatum that the missiles be dismantled and removed. The Soviet dictator yielded, and the missiles were removed. Russia, however, still maintains a military establishment in Cuba, which has become a Soviet satellite in the Western world.

For his decisive action, Kennedy was applauded by all the peoples of the Free World. Of him Walter Lippmann said in *Newsweek*, "he showed that he has not only the courage of a warrior, which is to take the risks that are necessary, but also the wisdom of the statesman, which is to use power with restraint."

Toward the end of Kennedy's third year in office, a marked improvement was brought about in relations between the West and the East. A treaty on limited testing of nuclear bombs was reached by Russia, Great Britain, and the United States. Following the signing of the treaty, there were further indications that Russia and the West were reaching an accommodation, even a *rapprochement*, the establishment of more harmonious relations. There were discussions on exchange of information between Russia and the United States in several areas where both nations would benefit. Tensions were relieved, and the world began breathing more easily.

While it is true that a position in the lineup of world leaders comes automatically to any man who takes up residence in the White House, only time and the record can tell how tall that man will stand among those leaders. Tragically, however, the Kennedy record was ended by an assassin's bullet on November 22, 1963. John Fitzgerald Kennedy was shot to death in Dallas, Texas, in the eleventh month of his third year in office. Stunned, the world and the nation mourned the passing of the youthful president. Tributes came from heads of state all over the world, many of whom came to the United States to attend the late president's funeral.

Kennedy's successor as the thirty-sixth President of the United States was Lyndon Baines Johnson, the man he had successfully battled for the presidential nomination four years before. President Johnson pledged himself to carry on the program Kennedy had launched but was never to finish.

It was strongly believed that John Kennedy would have been reelected to serve a second term as president had he lived. In his three years in office, Kennedy maintained a high degree of popularity. Many of his programs had not been passed by the Congress, but the United States was enjoying a high degree of prosperity and was at peace. Yet Kennedy himself, in his inaugural address, had said of his hopes and plans, "All this will not be finished in the first one hundred days. Nor will it be finished in the first one thousand days, nor in the life of this administration, nor even perhaps in our lifetime on this planet. But let us begin."

John Fitzgerald Kennedy began a program of high ideals. He was not permitted to finish it. Regardless of how historians regard the accomplishments of the fourth American President to be assassinated, John Fitzgerald Kennedy will be long remembered and long beloved.

Publisher's note: This book was about to go to press at the time of the assassination of President Kennedy. The last four paragraphs of this biography were written after the president's death.

NIKITA
KHRUSHCHEV

"WE WILL BURY YOU."

This remark was made by the dictator of one world superpower only a few months before he was the guest of the superpower which his nation—and its political philosophy—intended to inter.

The United States rolled out the red carpet for the speaker of these words and entertained him at the White House. Not that the United States took the words lightly. It does not take lightly any words spoken by Nikita Khrushchev, premier of Soviet Russia, a man with great power at his fingertips.

"I need only push a button," Khrushchev said quietly on one occasion, "and up you would go!"

When he made these two remarks, the leader of Red

Russia's millions was neither boasting nor threatening. He firmly believes what he says. To him, both statements are statements of fact. Communism, he is convinced, will eventually take over the world. On this subject, Khrushchev has swallowed his own Communist propaganda hook, line, and sinker. While it is true that Communism poses a threat to the whole world, there are other forces—the forces of the Free World—that diametrically oppose the spread of Communism with a combined strength as great, if not greater, than the might of Soviet Russia.

What type of man is this Russian who holds such tremendous power? His name and his face are as familiar as any man's in the world. Millions of words have been written about him. He has been variously described as a clown, a buffoon, an actor, a hayseed, a boor; at one time or another he has publicly played each of these roles. He is also described as a man of brutal hardness, a skilled, intelligent politician, a calculating gambler, a wily, cunning man who knows what he wants. And indeed, he has publicly displayed his right to all these appellations.

Khrushchev is also a maze of contradictions. He ominously rattles rockets, then signs a limited nuclear test ban treaty. He harshly criticizes British invasion of the Suez and at the same moment brutally crushes a revolt in Hungary. He openly threatens the West and in the same breath says that East and West must live in peaceful coexistence.

One word is used more often than any other in describing Nikita Khrushchev—the word is *calculating*.

Yet with all of his power, all his skillful political ability, and all his calculating intelligence, Khrushchev is not without his serious problems. He has them at home and he has them abroad. His role as leader of world Communism has been seriously challenged by Red China's leader Mao Tse-tung, and in the early 1960s the breach between Russia and Red China, the two great Communist powers, was widening. On the home front he is still beset by Russia's economic problems, particularly the farm problem. Russia, as powerful as the country has become since the Bolshevik Revolution of 1917, still does not have enough food to feed its 200,000,000 people well by Western standards.

Khrushchev's rise to the No. 1 position in the Soviet Union came about because of his insistence on an expanded farm program. At this time he was battling Georgy Malenkov and Viacheslav Molotov for the dictator's throne, left vacant in 1953 with the death of Joseph Stalin. The battle was to last five years before Khrushchev emerged the victor.

Malenkov, the stronger of Khrushchev's two rivals, wanted to concentrate Russia's efforts on the manufacture of consumer goods. Khrushchev was against this. "We need machines, not consumer goods," he said. "We have not solved the food problem. We need tractors, thousands of them, to grow more food."

On this issue Khrushchev risked his political life. The stakes were high, but Khrushchev has always been a gambler. He opened up wastelands. Tractors roared across them. Crops were planted. A bumper harvest was reaped. Khrushchev the gambler won his bet. What better way of gaining the support of the masses than by providing them with more food?

On March 27, 1958, five years after Stalin's death, Khrushchev became premier of the Union of Soviet

Socialist Republics. He had been first secretary of the Communist Party since 1953. Now he controlled both the party and the state, the first man to hold both top positions since Stalin.

Nikita Sergeyevich Khrushchev (Nee-KEY-ta Sir-GAY-yee-vitch Kroosh-CHOF) was born April 17, 1894 in the small village of Kalinovka, near Kursk, close to the Ukrainian border. His father was an illiterate miner, and he and his family were among the poorest of the rural population. Of Khrushchev's early years little is known, and what little information we have is confusing. Khrushchev himself has added to this confusion, for his own version of his boyhood and youth is subject to change every time he tells it.

From what has been unearthed, however, Khrushchev was a Jack-of-all-trades. He was a shepherd, a locksmith, a pipefitter, a factory hand, and a mechanic. Encyclopedia authority states that Khrushchev did not learn to read or write until he was twenty years old. This is disputed by many students of Khrushchev on the theory that any man with his great store of native intelligence must have been self-driven to learn to read and write before that time. It is known that in 1921 he attended a Communist Party high school. He was then twenty-seven years old.

In World War I, Khrushchev was drafted into the Czarist Army. After the Bolshevik Revolution in 1917, he joined the Red Army and fought in the ranks along the southern front.

Khrushchev became an active Communist *apparatshik* (Party functionary) sometime in the early 1920s. It cannot be said of him, as it was of Lenin, that he became a Communist because of his studies of Marx or of his deep belief in the Marxist ideology. He became a Communist and an active, ambition-driven worker because the Communist Party was the ruling party—the *only* party. It is the belief of Turner Catledge, managing editor of *The New York Times*, that Khrushchev uses the Communist ideology more as a tool than as a doctrine.

The former shepherd boy moved steadily up the Communist ladder. Along with his secondary education, he was thoroughly trained in Communism. He first directed Party activities in Stalino, a city of some 400,-000 in the Donets Basin. Next, he moved on to similar duties in Kiev, capital of the Ukraine. It was there that he met Lazar Kaganovich, general secretary of the Ukrainian Communist Party and, more importantly, a brother-in-law of Stalin. Kaganovich was quick to recognize the energy, devotion, and drive of young Khrushchev and he became his mentor. With the added prestige of having a leading Party boss's arm around his shoulders, Khrushchev gained steady promotion. Later, when Khrushchev reached the top, he rewarded the man who had helped him up the Communist ladder by exiling him in disgrace to a menial job in a cement factory in the Urals. Loyalty is not one of the Soviet dictator's assets.

In 1929, Khrushchev was assigned by the Party to take a two-year course at the Industrial Academy in Moscow. During those two years he was secretary of the student Party. On completion of his studies, Khrushchev became Party secretary—successively and successfully —in two important Moscow districts. In 1934 he was elected a member of the Soviet Communist Party's Central Committee.

The mid-thirties were years of danger and purges in the Soviet Union. Stalin, becoming more and more suspicious of anyone who posed even the slightest threat to his rule, liquidated opponents by the thousands. Nikita Khrushchev was not one of them, however. He remained close to Stalin, and his rise during those dangerous years was rapid. By 1938 he was the top Communist boss of the Ukraine, and a year later Stalin brought him into the inner circle of Communist leadership. Khrushchev became a member of the Politburo, now the Presidium, the nine-man committee that rules the Soviet. Although all nine members are supposed to have an equal voice in decision-making, Khrushchev's voice today is much more "equal" than any of the other eight members.

Little was known or heard of Khrushchev during his years as a close associate of Stalin. For that matter, Stalin saw to it that little was known of any of his top associates. Nor did he groom a successor; indeed, he quickly liquidated anyone who presumed to look toward that goal. What part Khrushchev took in the mass executions ordered by Stalin is not known, but Stalin demanded complete loyalty of his associates and if this was not immediately forthcoming, the associate was quickly done away with. It is unlikely that Khrushchev merely looked the other way as Stalin ruthlessly cut down his enemies, yet at the same time there is no proof that the younger man took an active part in the mass liquidations.

It has been said of Khrushchev during those years in the Kremlin that he was a "master of deceit with basic traits of craftiness and ruthlessness." A former Ukrainian professor who knew Khrushchev has been quoted as saying: "This man is utterly unprincipled, without a trace of Communist or any other kind of idealism. He has killed thousands, including his closest friends and comrades. Remember that only those for whom lying and brute force became second nature could rise under Stalin."

When Joseph Stalin died on March 9, 1953, there were four men who were looked upon as his possible successors. They were Lavrenti Pavlovitch Beria, head of the all-powerful Soviet secret police; Malenkov, the shrewd, ambitious bureaucrat; Molotov, Russia's skillful foreign diplomat and tough revolutionary; and Khrushchev. Four months after Stalin's death, Beria was liquidated, shot as a traitor.

Of the remaining three seekers for Stalin's job, Malenkov was given the best chance, Khrushchev the poorest. Everyone underestimated Khrushchev. People were even disdainful of the boisterous, boorish, crude former *muzhik* (peasant). He was called "Kukuruzhnik." which means "corn"; by that they meant he was a hayseed, a country bumpkin.

The fight for power went on for five years. Khrushchev moved first against Malenkov, aligning himself with Molotov to dispose of his rival. Thus Malenkov was the first to go, politically liquidated by the "country bumpkin" he once scorned. Now Khrushchev turned against Molotov, charging him with being wrong about the very things he supported him for when Molotov was his ally against Malenkov. Then Molotov went, demoted to a minor post in Siberia.

Khrushchev won and became the dictator of Soviet Russia on March 27, 1958.

The former shepherd, pipefitter, locksmith, and mechanic has come a long way from his poverty-stricken, peasant background. His picture is on the front pages of newspapers throughout the world. His actions, his pronouncements, are headline news.

The United States first saw this man in 1959 on his whirlwind visit here. As he and his party traveled from Washington to New York, through the cornfields of Iowa, on to Los Angeles and San Francisco, the nation saw a man who looked like anything but the head of a world superpower. They saw a squat, stocky man with the figure of a wrestler. Others said he looked more like a longshoreman than a head of state.

Khrushchev stands five feet, five inches tall and weighs 195 pounds. His head is round and nearly bald. He has been described as "remarkably ugly," with three prominent moles on his cheeks and two gold teeth behind a loose-lipped mouth. He has a rolling gait that reminds one of a bear. His heavy-lidded blue-gray eyes are piercing, and they are the best indicator of the Russian dictator's mood. From a warm twinkle of pleasure they can turn as cold as ice cubes when he becomes annoyed. He can change from friendliness to flaming anger with the abruptness of a finger snap. When Khrushchev visited the United States, Americans saw a man of many moods, as quickly changeable as they were numerous.

It was during this visit that he was reminded of his remark about the United States—"We will bury you." Khrushchev flared into anger and threatened to cut his visit short. By the following day, he showed no evidence of his outspoken annoyance and continued on his trip.

Khrushchev is desperately anxious to catch up with the United States, and this explains his "We will bury you" remark. As of 1963, Russia turned out less than half the amount of products the United States manufactured and grew. But it is said that Russia's rate of economic growth is twice that of America. Khrushchev is driving his country's workers toward a goal. He once said that by 1970 he intends that Russians will surpass the production output per person of that of the American worker. (Few, if any, Americans believe this.)

The United States next saw the Russian leader the following year on his visit to the United Nations in New York as head of the Soviet delegation. They saw him with his arm around the Cuban leader Fidel Castro. He also was seen by millions over television in a violent display of public anger, a desk-pounding, boisterous boor as he rudely interrupted any speaker whose words he did not like. He was even seen to take off a shoe and use it as a gavel to rap out his angry disagreement.

The Soviet leader brought the world close to World War III in 1962. He armed Cuba, which had become a Russian satellite, with Russian missiles and launching pads. These offensive weapons were capable of delivering nuclear warheads to any city in the United States. President Kennedy took immediate action. He demanded that the Soviet premier order the missiles dismantled and removed forthwith. The world trembled as it awaited Khrushchev's reply to this stern ultimatum. Khrushchev backed down and agreed to President Kennedy's terms. However, Russia still maintains military personnel and materiel in Cuba, and Cuba remains a Russian satellite.

Since that time, relations between the Soviet Union and the United States have improved. Many believe this to be the result of the ever-widening split between Russia and Red China. Where once Khrushchev and Mao Tse-tung, China's leader, were close friends and allies, they became enemies in the early 1960s. The split comes from a decided difference of opinion on the part of the two Communist leaders over how to overcome the capitalistic West, with particular reference to the United States. Mao believes that a war with the West is inevitable and that the only way is to destroy the United States, a country that he hates. As for Khrushchev, he has stated his belief that Communism can take over the world through the peaceful spreading of that doctrine.

President Kennedy's statement on this growing rift between the two Red powers (referred to in the chapter on Mao) is well worth quoting in full in connection with Khrushchev. President Kennedy said:

> What comfort can we take from the increasing strain and tension within the Communist bloc? Here hope must be tempered with caution for the Soviet Chinese disagreement is over a means, not ends. A dispute over how to bury the West is no ground for Western rejoicing.

Khrushchev speaks of living with the West in a condition of peaceful coexistence. While this sounds fine, political experts define his idea of peaceful coexistence as meaning to exist in peace the way Khrushchev wants it.

Toward the end of 1962, there was a definite improvement in Soviet-Western relations. A limited nuclear test ban treaty was negotiated by Russia, the United States, and Great Britain. It was signed by those three nations and numerous others throughout the world. This brought about a *détente* between the East and West, *détente* being a French word meaning the easing of tensions among nations. Thus the cold war became the "cold peace."

How sincere Khrushchev was in agreeing to limit nuclear testing to underground explosions, and how long he will live up to the treaty, was a matter for much speculation at the time the treaty was being negotiated. He is quite capable of taking unilateral action and starting to test nuclear bombs in the atmosphere, with no notice to the other signatories to the treaty. Indeed, he did this once before. An unofficial moratorium on nuclear testing was agreed upon during President Eisenhower's second administration. Khrushchev violated the moratorium with no advance notice, an action for which he received world-wide criticism.

In 1963, the Soviet leader turned sixty-nine and there was evidence that he was being confronted with the personal physical problems that come to most men at that age. He still has a tremendous capacity for work and a seeming overabundance of energy. His daily schedule is crowded. He still delivers two- and three-hour speeches, despite the fatigue that shows in his face and the report that he suffers from high blood pressure and a kidney ailment.

Whether this powerful dictator will live to attend the West's funeral is highly doubtful on two scores: one, he is growing old; two, and more important, the West shows no inclination to roll over and die. But Khrushchev will work toward the execution of his threat to bury us until he himself is interred.

HAROLD
MACMILLAN

THERE HAVE BEEN numerous occasions since he took office in 1957 when Great Britain's Prime Minister Harold Macmillan has been tagged with the label "good." At other times the label read "great," and at still others the label contained only a question mark.

At no time, however, whether the Prime Minister was riding high, low, or somewhere in between, has there been any doubt as to his being one of the most politically effective prime ministers in England's long history.

During Macmillan's tenure of office, Great Britain has been severely shaken by blows from outside her islands. Domestically, John Bull has been even more shockingly rocked by scandal in high places.

Through all these crises—international and domestic

—Macmillan, a tall, handsome, elegant man, has held a tight rein on his nation's destiny and steered her people and economy to a position of "you never had it so good," a phrase he used himself.

On one point concerning Macmillan, all observers agree, whether or not they support him—namely, as a politician Harold Macmillan is a real professional. When Macmillan became prime minister in 1957, he was exactly what England needed. Britain's position at that time was at a low ebb, both at home and abroad. The Suez Canal invasion had proved a fiasco. Her position with her long-time ally, the United States, was shaky. The United States had sharply criticized Britain for invading the Suez; in fact, the United States had even joined with Russia—an unprecedented union—in the United Nations, in voicing disapproval of the Suez action. The British economy was on the downslide and unemployment was up.

In Harold Macmillan Britain got just what she needed —an honorable man, a judicious man, an experienced man, an extremely professional politician who could tackle a great number of problems and solve them in a hurry.

None of the problems were easy ones. Few if any mistakes could be made. Or, if one were made, it would have to be of the most minor nature. One single, large mistake could bring disaster to the troubled nation.

Harold Macmillan saw to it that no large mistake was made, and even the small ones which beset his Tory government were handled with a dispatch that soon had them repaired and forgotten.

To the world at large, Macmillan's ascendancy to the highest office in the United Kingdom was somewhat of a surprise. He emerged from the shadow of England's great wartime prime minister, Winston Churchill, and the lesser shadow of Britain's famed wartime foreign minister Anthony Eden, who was also the prime minister whom Macmillan succeeded.

The image projected by Macmillan at first, particularly in the United States, was that of an old-line English aristocrat—which he is not, although he looks the part. A tall man—he is six feet one inch—he has a heavy, military mustache, neatly trimmed. His light hair is combed back somewhat carelessly. It is true that Macmillan comes from a wealthy family. He belongs to the right clubs and went to the right schools—Eton, and Balliol College of Oxford. His great-grandfather, however, was a Scottish crofter, or tenant farmer, on the island of Arran. Macmillan's grandfather, Daniel, was a book salesman who had known poverty in his earlier life. Together with his brother Alexander, Daniel Macmillan set up a bookshop in Cambridge. Later they moved to London, where they founded the great Macmillan book publishing house. The publishing business continued to thrive, and Harold's father, Maurice, joined the firm after a few years as a teacher at London's St. Paul's School for Boys.

Maurice Harold Macmillan was born in London on February 10, 1894. (He no longer uses the name Maurice.) His mother was an American, Helen Artie Belles, of Spencer, Indiana. Much has been made of the hands-across-the-sea makeup in Macmillan because of his American mother, just as it was about Winston Churchill, whose mother was also an American. Yet Harold Macmillan, despite his mother's nationality, is as "Saville Row" and "Berkeley Square" as any titled Englishman kneeling before his queen.

Macmillan was a member of the Grenadier Guards

during World War I and served with distinction. He was wounded three times, the third time when he was cut off from his own troops. It is said that when his troops found him in a foxhole a day later, he was reading a copy of Aeschylus in the original Greek. He remains an avid reader today. Macmillan spent over a year and a half in bed as a result of his third wound. His pelvis had been shattered and it was thought for a time that he would never walk again. For his war service, he was awarded the Military Cross.

After the war, Macmillan went to Canada as aide-de-camp to the governor general, the Duke of Devonshire. In 1920, he married the duke's third daughter, Lady Dorothy Evelyn Cavendish. That same year he became a director of the publishing firm of Macmillan & Co. Ltd., a position he held until 1940.

The future prime minister's entrance into politics came in 1923 when he "stood" (ran) for a seat in the House of Commons from Stockton-on-Tees in 1923. He lost in the first election but won handily the following year, and with short interruptions, held his seat until he became a cabinet minister.

Macmillan was a member of the Tory or Conservative Party, but was considered by old-line members to be a left-wing rebel. Winston Churchill himself was regarded in the same light, and the two were snubbed for many years by Tory leaders. Macmillan was highly critical of Conservative leadership, particularly as to the party's foreign policy. He was in vigorous disagreement with the Conservative government of Neville Chamberlain and opposed the Munich appeasement agreement with Hitler.

When Winston Churchill became Britain's wartime

prime minister, Macmillan was made undersecretary of state for colonies. From 1942 to 1945, he held the highly sensitive position of British resident minister at Allied Headquarters in North Africa. Following the war, the Conservative Party fell and the Labor Party took over. The Conservative Party was returned to power in 1951, and Macmillan became more prominent in the government. His first post was that of minister of housing and local government. In this position he made a brilliant record. One of the campaign promises made by the party was to build 300,000 badly needed new houses annually. It was believed that this campaign promise would go the way so many campaign promises go, but Macmillan rolled up his sleeves and the goal was achieved. Following this post, he served as minister of defense, secretary of state for foreign affairs, and then chancellor of the exchequer, until January, 1957, when he succeeded Anthony Eden as prime minister.

The picture of Macmillan the man became much clearer to Americans as the result of two television programs. The first appearance came a year after he assumed his high office. This was on Edward R. Murrow's "See It Now" show and revealed the prime minister's quiet humor, his original viewpoints, his modesty, and his warm, yet understated personality. Due to this appearance, he made millions of friends in the United States and increased his popularity in England when the show was repeated there.

Macmillan's second, and more dramatic television appearance in this country came at the 15th General Assembly of the United Nations in October of 1960. The tall, handsome Englishman took the floor and in a calm, controlled parliamentary manner, delivered a devastating attack on Russia's Nikita Khrushchev, who earlier in the session had viciously attacked Dag Hammarskjöld, the UN's secretary general. Macmillan's quiet, statesmanlike words drove Khrushchev to fist-pounding fury and shouted interruptions. Macmillan ignored them all, pausing only once to take note of the Russian leader's rude outbursts. "I should like that to be translated if he wants to say anything," Macmillan said quietly.

At the conclusion of his masterful address, the Assembly gave Macmillan the greatest applause to be given to any speaker at the meeting. Television viewers joined in at home. The Free World cheered the British prime minister for his bold, forthright speech.

The British lion had roared again, although the roar was in the words, not in the tone of Macmillan's mannered delivery.

Harold Macmillan emerged as a world figure, a world leader. He had come a long way from his early days in office. In his first months as prime minister, he had been withdrawn, closeting himself with the many problems facing his nation. Friends and associates were worried by his refusal to communicate with the public. A public opinion poll at this time showed him to be the most unpopular prime minister since Neville Chamberlain. At this time Harold Macmillan was called "Mr. Macmothballs."

Britain's problems—not his own popularity—were Macmillan's primary concern. Once he had these problems firmly in hand and had decided on a course to solve them, Macmillan tackled them with a swiftness that changed his nickname from "Mr. Macmothballs" to "Mac the Knife."

There were four major areas where action had to be taken and taken quickly. One was the stagnant British economy. It was not moving forward. In fact, it was teetering on a thin edge that could tip it downward to disaster. Macmillan's experience as chancellor of the exchequer thus proved invaluable. He knew where to go for advice, and as a professional politician, he knew how to take it. He surrounded himself with young, vibrant economists. He persuaded the British public to make small sacrifices for the present to gain large rewards in the future, and the economy began to move forward again. True, it remained in low gear at the start, but as the months went by, progress quickened. By the middle of Macmillan's sixth year as prime minister, Britain could boast of a sharp drop in unemployment, new export records, booming retail sales, and rising corporation profits.

A second troubled area was the breach that had widened between the United Kingdom and the United States as a result of Britain's disastrous invasion of the Suez, a loss that still rankled at home. To repair this breach and strengthen British-American relations, Macmillan turned to his wartime friend and associate, Gen. Dwight D. Eisenhower, then president of the United States. The volume of communication increased between the White House and No. 10 Downing Street, the prime minister's official residence. Exchange of opinions, discussion of policies on mutual problems narrowed the breach, until the historic closeness between the United States and Great Britain was re-established. This closeness continued with President Kennedy, and the two were often referred to as "Jack and Mac."

The British people had been badly shaken by the Suez defeat. This, combined with a shaky economy, had cause many Britons to lose faith in themselves, and here was a third area where Macmillan realized action must be taken. It is difficult to account for the methods by which any people regain faith in themselves. But they did in Great Britain. One reason, of course, can be ascribed to an improving economy. People with money in their pockets, with TV sets, washing machines, automobiles, are not likely to feel they have come to the end of the road. And the British public's lot is now a much better one than in pre-Macmillan days. Private ownership of automobiles in Great Britain doubled during Macmillan's tenure of office. Personal income has risen sharply. TV antennas stud British rooftops. Another indication of prosperity is gambling— the British are great bettors. In 1962, it was estimated that in the British Isles alone, $3,000,000,000 were wagered in one form of gambling or another.

Macmillan, with three troubled areas under control, turned his attention to closing the ranks within his own Conservative Party. Again, the Suez had been the main issue to split the Conservatives. Macmillan, a persuasive politician and a practical, rather than theoretical one, worked closely with members of the House of Commons. He was frank in his talks, tolerant toward compromise. He took to television, and his forthright, candid manner gained him friends and respect. He became popular on the "telly" (the British equivalent of "TV"). The opposition Labor Party saw Macmillan easily dispose of the small issues they brought up. The Conservative Party grew stronger.

But even with the restoration of England's faith in

itself, the improvement in its economy, the rewelding of British-American relations, and the strengthening of the Conservative Party, Macmillan's Conservatives have not had untroubled sailing. Twice the party was rocked by international setbacks.

One of these blows brought a crisis in Anglo-American affairs, despite the close relations the two nations were enjoying. It came about over a long-range missile called the Skybolt. This missile, developed by the United States, was capable of carrying a nuclear warhead to targets a thousand miles distant. It would be flown to within this range by long-distance bombers. Great Britain, which has no long-range missile program of its own, was to take the Skybolt for its own bomber force. But after the United States had spent $650,-000,000 on the Skybolt and it had proved unreliable, the program was scrapped. Great Britain felt it had been doublecrossed, since it had spent $25,000,000 in adapting its Vulcan II bomber to carry the Skybolt. The dispute raged in British headlines. Uncle Sam offered to aid Britain in adapting its nuclear submarines to carry Polaris missiles, and following a meeting between Macmillan and President Kennedy in Nassau, the British press turned its attention in another direction.

A second blow came to Great Britain when President Charles de Gaulle of France blocked Britain's entrance into the Common Market (European Economic Community). When the Common Market was first formed, England had been invited to come in. She refused. As the years went by and the Common Market proved itself an outstanding method of lifting the economy of Europe, Great Britain wanted to come in. A large segment of British opinion was for joining, although there

were those who still opposed. It was a blow, however, when Britain did evidence its desire to join the Common Market, to have de Gaulle shut the door. The French leader based his action on his assumption that Britain was too closely allied with the United States and the British Commonwealth to be truly European.

The two domestic blows to rock the Conservative government came in Macmillan's fifth and sixth years as prime minister. Both involved security. In the first case, a clerk in Britain's Admiralty was found transmitting naval secrets to the Russians. The second case caused the resignation of a member of Macmillan's cabinet, when the minister of defense for war admitted being involved with a woman who was also seen frequently in the company of a Russian naval attaché. This scandal was headline news for months and threatened to topple Macmillan's government. Many thought he would be forced to resign, but Macmillan handled the affair with his customary honesty and calmness. In a convincing talk to the British people on television, he said calmly that it was "something which has never occurred in my life before—a world unrevealed and quite foreign to me, and very unpleasant."

This simple, yet eloquent statement, carried great conviction for the British public. Macmillan had weathered another storm.

With Macmillan's participation in the negotiations leading to the signing of the limited nuclear test ban treaty by the United States, Great Britain, and Russia, his popularity was restored. Toward the end of his sixth year in office, in 1963, it appeared that the opposition would have to hold off for some time before putting into use its slogan of initials: "MMG"—"Macmillan Must Go."

Macmillan did resign in October, 1963. Not, however, because of increased strength on the part of the opposition party. Macmillan underwent a serious operation which forced him to resign as Britain's prime minister. It could be said, however, that he personally hand-picked his successor, Lord Home.

Harold Macmillan held no formal position in Great Britain's government after his resignation. He did continue to play an important though unofficial part in the political and economic destinies of the nation he served so long and so well.

MAO
TSE-TUNG

"MAKE A BIG NOISE in the East but strike in the West."
The man who is making that big noise is Mao Tse-tung. He has aroused China from its hundreds of years as a sluggish, sleepy dragon; he has inflamed its 700,-000,000 people into active hatred of the United States; he has dedicated himself to conquest of the world.

Mao Tse-tung (pronounced MAH-o DZU-DOONG), soldier, politician, scholar, and poet, is chairman of the Communist Party of the People's Republic of China. He holds no official government position such as head of state or commander-in-chief of the armed forces. He is simply Chairman Mao, but as such he is the absolute ruler of Red China's teeming, increasing millions.

The United States, labeled by the Chinese as the "arch enemy of world peace," is considered by Chairman Mao as the leading imperialist among all Western nations. He has declared that "should the imperialists start a war of aggression, we will certainly wipe them clean from the surface of the globe."

This "Hate America" propaganda line has been used effectively by the Red Chinese leader to weld his nation's people solidly behind him, in order to build China into a strong nation that is ready—even eager— to spread Communism throughout the world. Political power, Mao affirms, grows out "of the barrel of the gun." He has never hesitated to use the gun, but he has made certain that "the gun never commands the Party." The Communist Party, controlled by Mao, is in complete charge of the armed forces of China.

The Communist Revolution in China had its beginnings with the formation of the Chinese Communist Party in 1921. Mao was one of its twelve founding members. His entire life has been that of a revolutionary, and his activities have been a major, indispensable force in the success of the Revolution.

Mao's blazing career and the Revolution itself owe much to his peasant background and his hatred of his father, as well as to the conditions in China at the time of his birth and early years.

Red China's future leader was born on December 19, 1893 in the village of Shao Shan in Hsian T'an County of Hunan Province. He had two brothers and one sister, all younger than himself. Mao's father, Mao Jen-sheng, had been an extremely poor peasant, but after serving in the army he managed to pay off his debts, acquired three and one-half acres of land, and started a rice-trading business. This increase in the family's fortunes, however, did not bring about a decrease in the harsh treatment dealt out by the father to his family and servants. They continued to live in terror of Mao Jen-sheng's uncontrollable temper.

When only seven, frail and undersized for his age, Mao was forced to work in his father's rice fields. The father drove his eldest son and scorned him for his inability to keep up with older and stronger workers. On several occasions Mao ran away from home, only to return to defend his mother against his father's daily wrath.

Mao's dislike of Confucianism was sparked by his father. The laws of Confucius, set down twenty-five hundred years before, still governed family life in China. The father was the absolute ruler of the family. His word was law. His orders were to be obeyed instantly and without question. In his childhood Mao identified his father's authoritarianism with the precepts of Confucius, and in his later years he was to lead the fight to destroy Confucianism as a ruling force in China.

Hunan, the province of Mao's birth, had long been an area in central China where militarism was dominant and the law of the gun was ruthlessly enforced. In a single year, when Mao was only thirteen, he witnessed two insurrections, a riot of half-starved peasants against landlords, and a rebellion in his own home town which was quickly put down.

At the age of fourteen, Mao was married to a twenty-year-old peasant girl. This was an arranged marriage, with Mao's father selecting the bride and dictating his son's participation in the ceremony. Here was another example of the laws of Confucius against which in later years Mao was to lash out. This marriage, the first of four for the Chinese revolutionary, was never consummated.

In 1907 Mao left home to attend school in Hsiang-hsiang, a town fifteen miles from his home. His father gave reluctant approval to this move. He had wanted his son to be apprenticed to a rice merchant instead. At this school Mao, like millions of other young Chinese at that time, was taught to identify China's poverty and its corrupt political system with exploitation by Western powers. This early hatred of the West later became channeled almost exclusively against the United States.

Mao continued his education at a secondary school in Changsha, entering in 1911. That same year, although still doubtful about Sun Yat-sen's Kuomintang movement, he joined the Nationalist army and served for a year as an orderly to two officers younger than himself. After leaving the army, he enrolled in a tuition-free teaching college in Changsha—his father had long since stopped giving him any allowance. Mao remained in the college for six years, and during this period he first came upon the writings of Karl Marx, which were to shape his career as a world leader of Communism.

Graduating in 1918, Mao spent a year in Peiping— now Peking—as a lowly assistant in the Peiping University library, and he continued his studies in his spare time. He returned to his native province of Hunan in 1919, edited the *Hasian River Monthly Review*, and organized Hunan students in an attempt to overthrow the military governor of the province. The attempt failed, but Mao was launched on his long and successful career as a revolutionist.

The core of the Communist Party in China was formed by the May 4, 1919 student demonstrations in

Peking against provisions of the Treaty of Versailles. The demonstrators were protesting the granting to Japan of concessions in China formerly held by Germany. Mao was swept up in this movement and he attended the founding congress of the Communist Party in Shanghai in the summer of 1921.

Mao returned to Hunan after the founding congress adjourned, and there he established the Hunan Province branch of the Communist Party and organized a number of trade unions. This marked official recognition of Mao as a Communist leader. Although he experienced minor setbacks, he had started up the Red path toward the top position in the Chinese Communist Party, and as the party chairman, the recognized and undisputed head of the People's Republic of China.

In the early years of the movement, the Communists collaborated with the Kuomintang to form a united front against the warlords of northern China. The Kuomintang, a political party formed in 1912 with the establishment of the Chinese Republic, was still the ruling party of China. Mao became a member of the Kuomintang but continued to serve as a member of the central committee of the Communist Party. The collaboration of the two parties was broken off in 1927 when Chiang Kai-shek, director general of the Kuomintang, led a massacre of workers in Shanghai.

Mao, by now a confirmed follower of the principles of Karl Marx, saw in the millions of Chinese peasants the source of the revolutionary power needed to establish Communism in China. In this he departed from the Marxist principle that a revolutionary movement must come from the proletariat, or working classes, as distinguished from the peasant farmers.

In the fall of 1927, Mao led his first revolutionary

army in his first strike against the Kuomintang. His army of 2,000 Hunan peasants, many of them shoeless, was a pitifully underarmed force. There were only 200 rifles and not enough ammunition for them. The rest of the army was equipped with two-edged spears mounted on long, hand-hewn sticks. The uprising was unsuccessful. Mao and 1,000 survivors of his army fled to Chingkanshan Mountain in Kiangsi Province. Here he was joined in the spring of 1928 by Chu Teh, a former warlord who had become a Communist.

Mao as political commissar and Chu Teh as military commander, formed the Fourth Workers' and Peasants' Red Army. For the next few years, Mao and his army —growing ever larger—fought hit-and-run battles in the mountains, developing techniques of guerrilla warfare which have earned Mao his reputation as a proven authority on this type of battle. He even published a primer on guerrilla warfare in 1937.

By 1931, Mao had grown in power and was recognized as the outstanding leader of the Communist movement in China. In November of that year, the first national congress of soviets was held in Juichin in Kiangsi Province, where Mao's army was encamped, and the Chinese Soviet Republic was formally established with Mao as its chairman.

Chiang Kai-shek, alarmed at the growth of the Communist movement and at Mao's success in organizing and enlisting the peasants to his cause, began his "extermination campaign" against the Communists. Four times Chiang Kai-shek hurled his superior forces against the Red armies. Four times the peasant armies threw back the attacks.

In a fifth campaign, which lasted through most of

1934, Chiang Kai-shek was successful, dealing a crushing defeat to the Communist armies. This, for the Red armies, was the beginning of their "Long March," a celebrated retreat of 6,000 miles, considered by military experts to be one of the most extraordinary feats in the history of warfare.

One hundred thousand battle-weary Red soldiers started out on the Long March. Twenty thousand completed it. Chiang Kai-shek's troops pressed them all the way. Fifteen major battles were fought, and three hundred skirmishes. From Kiangsi, southwest of Shanghai, where the retreat began, to Yenan, far west of Peking, the Red armies climbed eighteen mountain ridges, forded dozens of rivers, and marched an average of fifteen miles a day, eating when food could be found, going hungry for days at a time.

Mao's leadership kept the bedraggled army together. One year and three days after the Long March began, the remnants of Mao's armies escaped the last attacks of Chiang Kai-shek's troops and found safety in Yenan Province. Mao's stature in the eyes of peasants and other Communist leaders increased tremendously. As the new year 1935 opened, Mao's authority in the party was supreme.

Headquarters for Mao during the next ten years was a cave in Yenan. Here he lived, raising his own tobacco —he is a chain smoker—writing, studying, and directing the operations of the Red armies and the Communist Party. Japan, which had invaded Manchuria in 1931, launched a full-scale attack on China in 1937. Forming an uneasy truce with Chiang Kai-shek, Mao's armies joined those of the Kuomintang in combating the invading Japanese forces. With the end of World War II and the defeat of Japan, Mao attempted to reach an agreement with the Kuomintang and set up a coalition government. Chiang Kai-shek treated Mao rudely and disdainfully. Mao complained bitterly of this treatment, saying Chiang Kai-shek had treated him "like a peasant."

At this time, Mao was severely criticized by members of his own party for being too soft with the Kuomintang and for offering too many concessions in his effort to establish a coalition government. Many Western political observers at this time looked upon Mao as being interested primarily in agrarian reform—that is, in dividing up agricultural lands into small units and giving them to peasants. He was also considered to be a man of strong democratic leanings. These opinions were to change, and change rapidly in the next ten years.

Negotiations with the Kuomintang broke off and once again China was ripped with revolution. Mao's armies struck at the Nationalist government—the Kuomintang—and city after city fell into Communist hands as the Red armies rolled relentlessly through all China. By the end of 1949, the Nationalist government had been defeated. Its leaders, including Chiang Kai-shek, fled to the island of Taiwan (Formosa), where Nationalist China still holds out with Chiang Kai-shek as its president. In Red China today, with its 700,000,000 people, Mao and the Communist Party are the sole rulers. Yet two years before his victory, Mao's home had been a cave.

In October of 1949 the People's Republic of China was proclaimed, with Mao Tse-tung as chairman of the Central People's Government. Two months later Mao left China for the first time in his life, to visit Joseph Stalin, premier of Soviet Russia. Mao had been strongly influenced by Stalin's policies. He had come under this influence as early as 1942 and adapted many of the Russian premier's tactics to his own uses. Mao launched the first of his "rectification" programs, aimed at tightening party discipline and getting rid of undesirable members within his own party. In this he was following Stalin's footsteps.

In the second year of the new People's Republic, China was on a war footing again. The Korean War broke out in 1950. Mao, fearing a free, anti-Communist country on China's eastern border, poured his troops into the northern part of Korea. The war was ended by a truce, dividing Korea into Northern and Southern Korea. Mao, however, claimed China's participation in the war as a major victory over the American "paper tiger."

The first ten years of the Chinese People's Republic—1949–1959—under Mao's firm Communist control, saw the Red dragon shake off its sluggishness and start its move toward becoming a world power. More and more peasants joined the Party as Mao promised them farmland. The Red armies became "universities" of Communism. This continued a policy established by Mao twenty years before with his first small, poorly equipped army. The principles of Communism and hatred of the West were drilled into the armed forces with the same vigor that was devoted to teaching the manual of arms.

Mao instituted more and more "rectification programs." Landlords lived in terror as Mao's forces attacked them. Those in opposition to Mao's policies were ruthlessly slaughtered. Mao himself admits that during the early years some 800,000 persons were liquidated. Other estimates put the number killed much higher. A United States congressional report stated that the number killed during the first decade of the new republic was 30,000,000, and an official Communist report made in 1951 spoke of 1,150,000 "native bandits" killed in the south-central region of China, one of but six administrative regions of the Republic. Millions of other Chinese became slave laborers. The United Nations put the figure at 25,000,000.

Mao's marriage law did away with prearranged marriages such as he had gone through at the age of fourteen. Child marriages were abolished—a man had to be twenty and a girl eighteen before they could marry. Women were given equal rights with men. The age-old social system of China was broken down—Confucius and his laws, under which China had lived for two thousand years, were replaced by Mao and Communist laws.

"The east wind is prevailing over the west wind," Mao the poet and phrasemaker said. "Western imperialists are paper tigers," is another phrase he uses to state his belief that while the United States and other Western powers look strong from the outside, they are weak inside.

As China grew stronger during these years, Mao began making an even bigger "noise" in the East. Under the guise of establishing "peaceful coexistence" with Tibet, Mao moved into that small, highly religious country to "liberate" it from Western imperialism. Chinese schools under army direction were set up in Tibetan towns. Thousands upon thousands of Tibetan children under the age of fifteen years were taken from their families and sent to China. Protesting parents were told that parents who refused to let their children go would be executed by Mao's order.

Thousands of lamas—the clergymen of Tibet—were

buried or burned alive. Others were beaten to death; still others were torn apart by trucks, hanged, shot, stoned, crucified. Mao had told the Dalai Lama that religion was "bad," and that because of it Tibet was a backward country and its population would decrease. Mao did much to bring about this decrease. At last, brutal Chinese military action forced the Dalai Lama, Tibet's spiritual leader, to flee his country and find haven in India.

In 1957, the threat of open revolt against his policies brought about a softened approach on the part of the Chinese leader. This was a period of economic depression and extensive crop failures for China. Mao asked critics of his government to speak out, to air their opinions. "Let a hundred flowers blossom," he called out in his best phrasemaking form. "Let a hundred schools of thought contend." Criticism of the government poured in, far exceeding all expectations. Mao's beautiful words had backfired on him, but he took care of that quickly. Police rule was re-established. Free criticism came to a sudden end, and critics of government policy were suppressed by force.

Further crop failures magnified the food needs of China's hungry hordes. With a yearly population increase of 13,000,000, the economic situation in China became desperate. Mao launched a new program in 1958, terming it the "big leap forward." Farm communes, state controlled and directed, were established throughout all China. They were modeled after a farm commune (which he called "Sputnik") set up under Mao's personal supervision. These communes were not successful, and three years later, in 1961, Mao in order to curb the angry rumbling of his peasants was forced to give the farmers a greater measure of freedom.

China is still riddled with economic problems. But

despite them, Mao remains a hero to the Chinese people. He is considered a "living Buddha" and cheered in song and story as "the people's great savior."

Under Mao the lot of the peasant has been improved, although the problem of balancing food supplies with population remains staggering. Health conditions have been greatly improved. Chinese cities, once filled with filth, are now almost surgically clean. Rats and flies have been eliminated. A million doctors, nurses, and pharmacists now tend the peasants, who formerly treated themselves with herbs and died. Government corruption has been stamped out. Almost all Chinese children now go to school. The illiteracy rate has been lowered. The wealthy warlords have disappeared. Twenty million new acres of farmland have been brought under cultivation. Total crop production has been increased by millions of tons—yet there is still a long way to go before there is enough food for millions of hungry mouths. Living standards, while still pitifully low according to Western standards, have been raised. All this has taken place under Mao and his Communist rule.

Mao, as leader of the world's most populous nation, must be given his place among the world's political leaders. It is believed by many in the Communist bloc of nations that Mao overshadows Russia's Premier Khrushchev as the ideological leader of the Communist world because he adheres more closely to the principles of Communism laid down by Marx and carried out by Lenin.

In the early 1960s, relations between the Soviet Union and Communist China began to cool. Western observers watch closely this widening rift, which has brought about a division within Communist movements

throughout the world. There are those who favor the Peking type of Communism over that of Moscow. However, since Communism is dedicated to world revolution and the overthrow of capitalism, differences of opinion on how to do this are small cause for rejoicing, as President Kennedy pointed out in his State of the Union speech in 1963.

As a threat to the West, Mao cannot be ignored. He rallies his people with his "Hate America" campaigns. His spokesmen have branded both former President Eisenhower and President Kennedy in equally vicious terms.

Mao considers the world to be a guerrilla battlefield on which tactics he developed can be applied to the underdeveloped countries of Asia, Africa, and Latin America and bring about the eventual destruction of the United States.

Delegations from China to Africa and Latin America reached flood stage in 1960. Speaking to a group representing fourteen countries from these areas, Mao said: "Our common enemy is U.S. imperialism. The struggles of the people in Cuba and Latin America have helped the Chinese people and the struggle of the Chinese people has helped the people of Cuba and Latin America. We should unite and drive U.S. imperialism from Asia, Africa and Latin America back to where it came from."

Time is running short for Mao and his dream of world conquest. In 1963 the Red Chinese leader was sixty-nine years old. His close associates, though, in running China, are firmly united behind him. It is not believed that Mao's death will bring about the internal struggle for leadership that followed the death of Premier Stalin in Russia, resulting in Khrushchev's taking over.

As a person, Mao has always lived a simple, modest, even drab life. He has shown no interest in personal enrichment. He does enjoy good food and wine, and smokes as many as five packs of cigarettes a day. He has been married four times. His second wife was killed by Nationalist forces during Chiang Kai-shek's early drive against Communism. There is some mystery surrounding Mao's third wife, a former schoolteacher. It is believed they were divorced and she is living in Russia. Five children resulted from this union. Some of them—it is not known how many—had to be abandoned during the Long March. Mao's fourth marriage was to movie star Nan P'ing. Often Mao roams the country, visiting peasants. On these trips he dresses plainly in a drab uniform carrying no insignia of rank. Mao is a strong believer in physical fitness. At the age of sixty he swam the Yangtze River from Wuchang to Hankow three times.

Mao, despite his methods, has unquestionably hammered China into a nation to be reckoned with. In some areas he has advanced China much farther than any leader before him and in a considerably shorter time. If China's present rate of progress continues, either under Mao or Mao's successors, it is believed that in ten to twenty years China will stand with the current giants, the United States and Russia, as a full-fledged third world power.

GAMAL ABDEL NASSER

POLITICAL RELATIONS among the Arab nations of the Middle East have been as shifting as the sands which cover much of the wide desert areas of those countries. Unions between nations have been forged, only to be dissolved. This on-again, off-again quality has been typical of the movement toward a federation of Arab states for many years. At one time or another, Egypt, Syria, Iraq, and Yemen have either been joined in a United Arab Republic or have announced their intentions to form such a union.

Throughout these troubled years one man has stood firm in his efforts to cement these shifting political sands into a concrete confederation of Arab states. A firm union of Arab countries has been the long-time dream, the long-time goal of Gamal Abdel Nasser, president of Egypt. He has come close to the realization of this goal on several occasions, only to see it escape his grasp as assassination, revolution, or shifts in power in various Arab countries upset this dream.

Nasser's path toward Arab unity is strewn with road-blocks on his home front. Egypt's economic problems have been monumental. Hunger, poverty, disease, and a rapidly increasing population pile problem upon prob-lem for Egypt's president. Solving these problems must be Nasser's first concern.A strong, prosperous, healthy Egypt would prove to the Arab world that Nasser has the ability to weld the Arab nations into a strong union and to be that union's leader.

(Often in news reports Egypt is called the "United Arab Republic," another of its official names. This sec-ond name should not be confused with Nasser's ultimate dream of a firm federation of all Arab nations.)

Since 1952, Nasser—and Nasser alone—has been the outstanding leader of the Arabic world. His firm leader-ship of his own country has been steadfast, where leaders in other Arab countries have come and gone as revolu-tions swept their countries. Egypt's government is stable. Nasser has no challenger for his presidency. His power will decline only if he fails to raise his people from the substandard living which has been their lot for centuries.

This staggering task becomes readily apparent with the realization that 27,000,000 Egyptians crowd an arable land area no larger than the state of Maryland. To double the standard of living (as Nasser has prom-ised) under Egypt's depressed conditions would seem to be a sufficiently overwhelming, even lifetime job for any man. But Nasser's dream of an Arab empire never leaves his mind.

Gamal Abdel Nasser (NAS-ser) was born January 15, 1918 in Alexandria and grew up in the small town of Beni Mar in Asyut Province in Upper Egypt. He was the oldest of four sons. His father was a post office civil servant.

Nasser demonstrated his rebellious traits at an early age. Forbidden by his father to dig in the garden, Nasser, only seven, dug a hole so deep that his father fell into it.

The future president of Egypt had little interest in schooling as a young boy. He spent more time at the movies—American movies—than he did in the classroom. As he grew older, he became more serious. When he was sixteen, he led fellow students at Cairo's Al Nahda Al Misria school in a demonstration against Great Britain's domination in Egypt. His outspoken hatred of colonialism, expressed early and often, remains with him today.

After three years of law study and exhaustive reading of the biographies of great men, Nasser, then nineteen, entered the Royal Military Academy in 1937. He was graduated a year later and joined the Third Rifle Brigade as an infantry platoon commander. Again Nasser showed his rebel spirit. Considering the senior officers lazy, corrupt, and unqualified to lead, he organized the junior officers in successfully defying their commands.

After a year with the Third Rifles, Nasser became an instructor at the Royal Military Academy, then continued his studies at the Army Staff College in Cairo. While there, he learned all there was to know about secret military plans for the protection of Cairo against ground and air attack. He put this knowledge to active use later as leader of the military junta which overthrew King Farouk, ruler of Egypt.

Egypt was neutral during World War II, but Nasser

was an observer at El Alamein when British troops ended the Nazi threat to seize control of the Suez Canal.

In 1948, Nasser fought in the short-lived war against the new Republic of Israel. Egypt suffered a humiliating defeat in this war, but Nasser emerged a hero. He was wounded in the shoulder at the Battle of Faluja, and his bravery in action earned him the name of "Tiger of Faluja."

Nasser's long-smoldering ambition to overthrow the Egyptian monarchy was further inflamed during the Egyptian-Israeli war. He felt the major reason for Egypt's defeat should be blamed on the rulers in Cairo. Supplies had been inadequate, ammunition short, weapons were outdated. The fault lay, he believed, with the decadent rule of young King Farouk.

This belief that Egypt would forever remain a backward country under the monarchy was nothing new in Nasser's life. Overthrow of the monarchy had been in his mind since 1942. But he did not move rashly or try to rush his plans into execution. His thoroughness in planning is seen in the ten years he took to select, train, and indoctrinate the young officers he enlisted in his cause. He formed the Free Officers Movement, a body of seven hundred young men who became dedicated to the overthrow of the monarchy. The activities of this group were one of the best-kept secrets of any revolutionary movement in history. Only Nasser knew the names of all members, and very few members knew the names of their associates.

After the war with Israel, the seven hundred men infiltrated the palace and key positions in other sections of the government. When it was time to strike, Major General Mohammed Naguib was selected as leader of the Free Officers Movement. He was selected more as a "front man" than anything else. General Naguib had the respect of the Egyptian people as head of the army in the war against Israel, and even though Egypt lost, he had emerged as a strong man.

On July 23, 1952, Nasser struck his blow. In a bloodless *coup d'état*, the military junta headed by Nasser overthrew King Farouk. Farouk's seventeen-month-old son was named King Ahmed Fuad II, and General Naguib became premier of Egypt, but Nasser, still head of the military junta, was the power behind the throne. A year later, Egypt was proclaimed a republic, and the baby king was ousted. Naguib remained as premier, but Nasser held key positions in the new republic. He was minister for internal security, and more importantly, leader of the Revolutionary Command Council (RCC) —the military junta.

Although Naguib had been made premier of the new republic, more or less as a figurehead, the general refused to act like one. A power struggle developed between Nasser and Naguib. Nasser won. In April, 1954, Nasser became premier of Egypt, and Naguib was given the ceremonial title of president. Naguib still refused to take a back seat, so in November of the same year, he was deposed as president and left public office. He was under house arrest for several years.

Nasser had grown in stature since the proclamation of the Republic of Egypt. His handling of the years-long dispute between Great Britain and Egypt over the Suez Canal brought him great popularity at home and acclaim abroad.

The Suez Canal is a hundred-mile-long strip of water connecting Port Said on the Mediterranean Sea with

Suez on the Red Sea. It is the shipping lifeline, a super-waterway for trade, between Europe and the East. Use of the canal eliminates the long passage around the Cape of Good Hope at the tip of Africa.

Operation of the canal was in the hands of a company which had a 99-year concession lasting until 1968. Great Britain was the major shareholder in the company.

For seventy-two years British troops had occupied the Suez Canal Zone. This had been a festering thorn in Egypt's side. Nasser was the chief negotiator in settling this dispute. On July 27, 1954, Egypt and Great Britain came to an agreement for the withdrawal of British troops from the Canal Zone. Nasser's handling of the matter was hailed as "one of the most important diplomatic feats of the postwar period." Nasser himself called it "the turning point in the history of Egypt."

Two years later, Nasser was to take even more dramatic action in connection with the canal. His move startled the world and brought a war to the Middle East that threatened to blaze into a third world war. In June of 1956, the last British troops were pulled out of the Canal Zone according to the agreement. One month later Nasser, now president of Egypt, seized the Suez Canal and nationalized it.

This defiant action on Nasser's part came just a week after the United States announced it was withdrawing from its agreement to aid Egypt in building the Aswân High Dam. This was a staggering blow to Nasser, one he could not take without retaliation if he was to continue as Egypt's leader.

Nasser had promised Egypt the Aswân Dam. It was to be the salvation of Egypt. To be constructed 400 miles south of Cairo, it would be the world's largest dam with a reservoir 350 miles long. Two million acres of arable land would be added to Egypt's desperately needed farmland. Not only was the dam needed for Egypt's economic uplift, it was to be a striking symbol of Egypt's progress.

The dam would cost $1,300,000,000 and take ten years to build. Egypt needed financial help to build it. The United States, Great Britain, and the World Bank were approached for help. Negotiations went slowly. Egypt announced it would appeal to Russia for aid. To prevent this, and to keep Russian influence out of Egypt, the United States agreed to put up a large part of the capital needed. But when it became clear that Russia did intend to aid in the construction of the dam, the United States reversed its position and abruptly withdrew its offer of aid.

Nasser seized the canal. He announced that the $30,-000,000 in yearly receipts from the canal would be used toward defraying the cost of building the dam.

War clouds hung over the Middle East. Even before seizure of the dam, Nasser had refused the use of the canal to all shipping going to Israel. In October of 1956, Israel unleashed an attack on Egypt. Great Britain and France, their shipping through the canal shut off, bombed Egypt, and British and French troops invaded the land.

Rapid, effective action by the United Nations prevented the conflict from growing into an all-out war involving other countries. The United Nations called for a cease-fire, and the war came to an end as suddenly as it had started. A United Nations police force supervised the end of hostilities and took over the patrol of the Canal Zone.

Israel had badly defeated the Egyptian forces, and

France and Britain had inflicted severe damage in Egypt.
It appeared that Nasser and his country had suffered still
another humiliating defeat. But when the war ended,
Nasser still held control of the important waterway, although Israeli-owned ships once again were permitted to
use the canal.

The canal had been blocked from all shipping for the
five months from November, 1956, to March, 1957.

In July of 1958, an agreement was reached between
Egypt and the company holding the concession to the
operation of the canal, whereby the company would be
compensated for the remaining years of its concession.

Control of the canal remained in Nasser's hands. The
Suez was once again opened to world shipping, although
Nasser still hampered shipping to and from Israel by
seizing cargoes and delaying Israel-bound ships. Nasser
justified this action on the grounds that Egypt and Israel
were still at war.

To much of the world it appeared that Nasser had
suffered a defeat. United Nations police were control-
ling the Gaza strip, previously held by Egypt. Israel had
won a second struggle with Egypt. But to the Egyptians
and seventy million other people of the Arab world,
Nasser was a hero. He had been the one Arab to defy
the great powers of the world and win out against them
by retaining control of the Suez Canal. Nasser's name
was magic in the Arab world.

Self-assurance settled on him like a mantle and he
wears it well. His personal appearance is as impressive as
his actions. A six-footer, powerfully built, he has bold
features, deep-set dark eyes, a hawk-like nose, a clipped
mustache, and short black hair turning gray at the
temples.

Impressed by Nasser's leadership, neighboring Syria made a move to join Egypt in a United Arab Republic. For the eleven years of its independence, Syria had been rocked with twenty-one different cabinets, four constitutions, and six military coups bringing about changes in government. On February 1, 1958, the United Arab Republic was proclaimed, a union between Egypt and Syria. Nasser was named president and Syria's former president, Shukru el-Kuwatly, vice-president. A month later, Yemen joined the United Arab Republic, but she did not yield as much of her sovereignty as Syria had. This federation became known as the United Arab States.

It seemed that Nasser's long-time dream of Arab unity was approaching reality. But other Arab states did not come along. Iraq and Jordan, fearful of Nasser's growing power, formed their own Arab Federation, with King Faisal of Iraq as its head. This union was of brief duration. King Faisal was assassinated during the summer of 1958, and the Federation was dissolved.

Nasser's United Arab Republic fell apart in September, 1961, when Syria pulled out. Although remaining pro-Arab, the governing faction within Syria became anti-Nasser. Syria became again an independent nation. Yemen also pulled back from its association, although remaining more friendly toward Nasser.

It appeared in 1961 that Nasser's dreams of an Arab empire were at an end. But the off-again status became on-again in 1963. It was announced in April, 1963, that a new United Arab Republic was to be formed. Syria would come back into the union; Iraq would also join. By the fall of 1963, Yemen and Algeria were still considering their invitations to make it a five-state union.

Although once again Nasser's goal of Arab unity seems to be approaching reality, his problems in Egypt remain monumental. The Aswân Dam is under construction, with Russian aid, and Nasser can also claim other advances for the republic he has led since 1952.

One of Nasser's first moves was toward land reform. Half of Egypt's fellaheen, or peasants, owned no land at all. Two million farmers plowed a substandard living from one-acre plots of land. Therefore Nasser's republic seized 600,000 acres of farmland from wealthy, large landowners for redistribution among the fellaheen. A law was passed limiting farmland ownership to no more than 200 acres per family. Over 90,000 small farmers benefited from this first step toward land reform. Completion of the Aswân Dam will further relieve Egypt's desperate need for farmland, but with a fast-increasing population, Egypt will still have a struggle to raise enough food for its needs.

Agricultural improvement, although it is Egypt's first need, is not enough if the nation is to increase its standard of living. Realizing this, Nasser has called for industrial expansion in his country. Under a five-year plan, aimed at an annual increase of 10 percent in industrial production, a steel factory has been built, and a new oil pipeline, handling oil from newly built refineries, now runs between Cairo and Suez. Small factories, manufacturing electrical appliances, china, ceramics, auto tires, and other small products, have sprung up.

Much of the financial aid for Nasser's five-year plan came from the United States and Russia. One of Nasser's special talents seems to be his ability to secure aid from both the Western Bloc of powers and the Soviet Bloc without committing his nation to either side.

Improvement in health conditions has been slow but steady. New aqueducts have been built to provide clean, sanitary water, one of Egypt's greatest needs.

Improved living and health conditions, small as they have been, have contributed to Nasser's problems. The death rate has dropped, while the birth rate has risen.

In education, Egypt for hundreds of years lagged far behind. Prior to Nasser's regime, the government had allotted only 2 percent of its national budget toward education. This figure was upped to 15 percent by Nasser. Still, Egypt as a whole has an illiteracy rate of 75 percent. In the smaller villages illiteracy rises to 95 percent.

Progress has been slow in all areas, but there has been sufficient advancement in social and living conditions to make the Egyptian people hunger for more. Nasser must satisfy this hunger. By his actions on the home front, Nasser can continue to be the strongest leader in the Arab world. This is his first test, and his most difficult one. His second test, unification of the Arab peoples into a United Arab Republic, his ultimate goal, may not come in his lifetime. But he will be remembered as the man who charted the course.

JAWAHARLAL NEHRU

JAWAHARLAL NEHRU was the leader of India for nearly two decades. And during the twenty years before India achieved her independence (1947), he was in the vanguard of his country's struggle to break the bonds chaining her to the British Empire. His name and his actions have made international headlines for a generation.

Yet this leader of the nation with the second largest population in the world remains an enigma, a puzzling figure in a world where modern communications report almost daily on the activities of its leaders.

There is no question as to who Nehru was—he was the prime minister of the Republic of India, a nation of nearly 440,000,000 people. But there is no easy or quick answer as to *what* he was. Any answer inevitably leads to additional questions.

Nehru was one of the most important men in 20th-century history. There is little doubt as to his greatness as a leader of India. But as the years went by, Nehru's position as a world leader became subject to questioning.

Nevertheless newspapermen, political experts, and historians never fail to register him high on any list of the greatest leaders of the modern world. He has been described as "one of the towering figures of the world today"; "one of the most remarkable men of the 20th century"; "a man for the ages."

All these things—and more—have been said about Nehru. He remains a puzzle, however, for his position in the Cold War. In times of world crises, wherever they arose, Nehru's opinions and stand were eagerly sought after. Quite often they were as cloudy as they were disappointing. He condemned political action by one power bloc while condoning or being hesitant about speaking out against a similar action by another power bloc.

For the first fifteen years of India's independence, the one consistent and outstanding position of Nehru was neutralism. India, Nehru said, would be the leader of nations forming a neutral bloc between the military powers of the East and West in the Cold War. Nehru's stand of nonalignment with either bloc—although accepting aid from both—was the one firm position for which he was recognized.

But even this position became shaky when Red China attacked Indian borders in 1962. Nehru was then forced to turn to the West for military assistance, and since then India's alignment with the West has been definite, although it was never publicly stated by the Indian leader.

In the past Nehru had pleaded for Red China's admission to the United Nations, and India refused to go along with a United Nations vote branding China as the aggressor in the Korean War. Once upon a time the people of India chanted, "Hindi Chini bhai bhai!" (Indians and Chinese are brothers.)

Despite Chinese depredations of India's borders, Nehru did not change his basic belief in nonalignment, even if his people did. He always felt that nonalignment was good for India and for world peace. "The danger to world peace," he said, "is greater if the world is divided into two major groups. It is better to have a third force."

Nehru's devotion to neutralism, nonviolence, and nonalignment can be traced back to his long and close association with Mahatma Gandhi, India's great spiritual leader, who was called the "soul of India." Side by side these two men led India in her long struggle for freedom.

Before Nehru was associated with Gandhi, he had led a restless, although easy, life of luxury as a member of one of India's wealthiest and best families—a socially prominent family and a member of the Brahmin caste, the top class group of India's teeming millions.

Jawaharlal Nehru (pronounced Jah-WAH-har-lahl NAY-roo) was born on November 14, 1889 in Allahabad, in the United Provinces of northern India. His father was Motilal Nehru, a Kashmiri Brahmin and one of India's most distinguished lawyers. Nehru's boyhood was a lonely one. He had no friends his own age, and his closest associates were his governess and an English tutor,

Ferdinand T. Brooks, who had a great influence on young Nehru.

In 1905 when he was sixteen, Nehru's family took him to England, where he was entered at Harrow, one of England's finest preparatory schools. From Harrow he went to Trinity College of Cambridge University. He received his degree in 1910, then spent two more years at the Inner Temple in London studying law.

Nehru returned to India in 1912, a somewhat mixed-up young man. "I had become a queer mixture of the East and West," he wrote at the time, "out of place everywhere, at home nowhere."

His restlessness and his desire to identify with his homeland led him to enter politics. He became a moderate in the Indian National Congress Party, a member of the Home Rule League and of the All-India Home Rule League. At this time, Nehru and his father were far from close. Motilal Nehru was a conservative, while his son Jawaharlal tended to a more radical position.

In 1916, Nehru was married to a girl of seventeen named Kamala. This marriage was arranged, as was the custom in India at the time. The couple's honeymoon was spent in the beautiful valley of Kashmir, the ancestral home of both. The marriage, even though Nehru had not known Kamala before, developed into a beautiful relationship based on love and close understanding.

During World War I, the British demanded that India furnish troops to help in the battle against Germany. This demand was bitterly resented in India, intensifying India's desire for home rule. Following the war, in which thousands of Indians fought bravely and fiercely for Great Britain, the movement for Indian independence was stepped up. Unrest became widespread. Then India found its leader. He was Mahatma Gandhi. Nehru described Gandhi's emergence as India's leader in these words:

> And then Gandhi came. He was like a powerful current of fresh air that made us stretch ourselves and take deep breaths; like a beam of light that pierced the darkness and removed the scales from our eyes; like a whirlwind that upset many things, but most of all the working of people's minds. He did not descend from the top, he seemed to emerge from the millions of India. The essence of his teaching was fearlessness and truth, and action allied to these, always keeping the welfare of the masses in view.

Young Nehru became a devoted follower of Gandhi, who also drew Nehru's father into his movement. Father and son thus became close to one another, ending the cold reserve between them after many years. In 1922, both father and son were imprisoned for six months for their participation in Gandhi's civil resistance campaigns. This was not to be the only jail sentence served by Nehru as he worked with Gandhi for India's independence. In all, Nehru served ten years in prison before India gained her independence.

Nehru spent much of his time between prison sentences traveling all over his homeland. What he saw was a revelation to a young man of a wealthy background. He found that 400,000,000 of his fellow countrymen were living in abject poverty, ridden by disease and unable to read or write. Houses were shaky shambles or crude mud huts. Water was polluted. Seventy-five percent of all babies died at birth or within a few months. Misery was the daily lot of the people of India.

> "Looking at them and their misery," [Nehru wrote] "I was filled with shame and sorrow— shame at my own easygoing and comfortable life and our petty politics of the city, which ignored this vast multitude of semi-naked sons and daughters of India, sorrow at the degrada- tion and overwhelming poverty of India. A new picture of India seemed to rise before me, naked, starved, crushed, and utterly miserable."

Nehru's dedication to India's cause, her struggle for independence and for a better way of life, became his crusade. He redoubled his efforts. He became Gandhi's chief lieutenant. During this period he was secretary of the All-India Congress, its principal speaker and or- ganizer.

Throughout the 1930s, much of Nehru's time was spent in jail. Tragedy came to him three times during this period. His father, who had also spent many years in prison, died in 1931. Next came the death of his wife. At her funeral, Nehru was handed a red rose. He wore one in her memory until his own death, wherever he went. Nehru's mother died two years later. Both women had worked with Nehru. Both had been im- prisoned for their activities in behalf of India.

When World War II broke out, India once again be- came a reluctant member of the Allied forces through Great Britain's insistence. Gandhi, the accepted leader of India, announced his willingness to aid if Britain would grant India independence. In August of 1942 the "Quit India Resolution" was passed by the Indian Congress. This resolution demanded an end to British rule. A nationwide passive resistance campaign was launched by Gandhi. More than ten thousand Indians were killed during this campaign, and more thousands imprisoned.

Nehru was one of the first to be jailed. He was not released until June 15, 1945, the longest continuous prison term he ever served. The war in Europe had ended five weeks before Nehru was freed. A new government had come into power in Great Britain, and it announced that India would be given self-government. Independence was to be granted India in August, 1948, although later that date was moved closer—August 15, 1947. The biggest problem was whether India should become one nation or be divided into two. Members of the Moslem faith insisted they should live in a country of their own, with their separate religion and separate culture. This was strongly opposed by the Hindus and the Sikhs, who made up by far the most numerous group of India's population. A partition was agreed upon, although Gandhi opposed it. Nehru reluctantly agreed to the partition, which established a Pakistan carved out of a large territory in western India and another Pakistan, smaller, from eastern India.

Some 15,000,000 people moved from Pakistan to India or from India to Pakistan in the largest mass migration and resettlement in history. More than 200,000 lost their lives in the two-way movement.

The partition resulted in one of India's largest problems, one that still continues. Both India and Pakistan claim sovereignty over Kashmir, Nehru's ancestral homeland. The dispute remains unsettled today.

India's independence was proclaimed at midnight on August 14, 1947, and Nehru became the new nation's prime minister and minister for foreign affairs. However, India elected to remain a member of the British Commonwealth of Nations. Gandhi remained the spiritual leader of India.

Hardly had the country begun its new life as an independent nation when a great tragedy struck. Riots between Hindus, Sikhs, and Moslems over the partitioning became widespread. Mahatma Gandhi, grievously troubled as Indian fought against Indian, visited towns and cities all over India in an attempt to bring the riots to an end. He began another hunger strike, saying he would take no food until the riots were ended. Physicians said the seventy-nine-year-old leader could not last six days. At the end of the fifth day of his fast, Gandhi was so weak he decided to end his fast. He left his house to attend a prayer meeting. On his way, the great leader of India was cut down by an assassin's bullet.

All India mourned its great loss. Nehru said:

> The light has gone out of our lives and there is darkness everywhere. . . . The light has gone out, I said, yet I was wrong. For the light that shone in this country was no ordinary light. The light that illumined this country for these many, many years will illumine this country for many more years, and a thousand years later, that light will be seen in this country and the world will see it. . . .

Nearly a million people came to the cremation ceremonies of their great and beloved leader. None mourned

Gandhi's death more than Nehru. He was now alone as India's leader, and the problems confronting him—and which still confront India—were staggering.

The magnitude of the problems in India can be realized when only a few statistics concerning the nation's people and its economy are reviewed. India's population in 1963 was placed at nearly 440,000,000, with an annual increase of at least 9,000,000—nine million additional mouths to feed each year in a nation which has never had an adequate diet. The life span of the average Indian—the number of years he can expect to live—is placed at the shockingly low figure of 32 years. The average annual personal income for Indians in 1961 was $65, as against a $2,400 average in the United States. The illiteracy rate in India, when she became an independent nation, was 85 percent. It has since been reduced to 75 percent, but is still one of the highest in the world.

Nehru's efforts to raise India's standard of living were noble ones, applauded by all the world. He had much financial help in grants and loans from many countries. The United States alone has contributed some $4 billion to India; Great Britain $3 billion. West Germany contributed an enormous steel complex enabling India to increase its steel output from 1,500,000 to 3,500,000 tons yearly. (The United States produces 100,000,000 tons yearly.) Russia has contributed nearly $1 billion in aid in various forms.

Two five-year plans were launched by Nehru to improve conditions in India. The first one was devoted to agricultural reforms—irrigation, land reclamation, and improvement in community living. The core of India's living is in some 500,000 small villages; only 23,000 of them have electricity. Indian farmers are able to take only a small proportion of the potential yield from their land.

This first plan brought noticeable results, but left India still far short when living standards were compared to those in other nations, even some of the newer ones which were as underdeveloped as newly independent India.

India's second five-year plan saw allocations stepped up in all areas of the nation's economy, with greatly increased emphasis on industrialization. A third five-year plan was begun in 1962, with the main emphasis returning to agriculture because of the nation's desperate need for food. It is estimated that by 1966, India's population will reach the 500,000,000 mark.

In India, Nehru was the leader of a revolution in his own country, just as he was one of the leaders of the struggle to gain his nation's independence. He had to fight against ignorance and superstition. He had to lead his people out of age-old ways. He had to awaken India to 20th-century methods and ways of living. This was Nehru's biggest job, his revolution on the home front, and one which still faces India today.

In world affairs, Nehru stood for neutralism, peace, and nonviolence. But this image of the man changed radically when in December, 1961, Indian military forces invaded and captured the three tiny enclaves of Goa, Damão, and Diù. (An enclave is a foreign territory surrounded by another country.) These pin-point spots on the world map had been colonies of Portugal for over four hundred years. With forces of overwhelming size compared to those of the defenders, India swept over the enclaves and took possession of them in three days

Nehru was sharply criticized for his military action

especially because he had symbolized the man of peace for so many years. This was a complete about-face.

During the last few years of his life his stand on many world-shaking events was puzzling. He criticized the United States for its intervention in Cuba. He condemned the British and French for sending troops to the Suez Canal at the time of Nasser's takeover of the canal. Yet, when Russia crushed the Hungarian revolt with tanks and guns, the world waited for Nehru's condemnation of this action. It was slow in coming and not as sharp as the world expected from this supporter of the suppressed.

Nehru's image as "the world's conscience," his role of moral leadership, was seriously damaged by his action against Goa and his puzzling, almost vacillating stands at the time of many world crises.

The invasion of Indian borders by Red China in 1962 put Nehru in still another light. Even in India, where he remained the idol of his nation, questions were asked about many of his decisions. Once, however, no one dared question his leadership.

In the Western world, India is still regarded as the greatest force for stemming the tide of Communism in Asia, and Nehru, during his lifetime, remained the great symbol of neutralism for millions throughout the world.

However, on May 27, 1964, death took the disciple, Nehru, as it had taken the master, Gandhi, sixteen years before. A stunned Indian Parliament heard the announcement of the Prime Minister's death in the same words Nehru had used to inform India of the death of its great leader Mahatma Gandhi:

"Life is out. The light is out."

Under a burning midday sun, some three million Indians followed the gun carriage carrying Nehru's body through the streets of New Delhi. Men moaned and women shrieked their sorrow. Flowers and holy water were scattered before the funeral procession.

On the banks of the holy Jamuna River, where Gandhi had been cremated, the body of Prime Minister Jawaharlal Nehru was placed upon a sandalwood pyre covered with roses, marigolds, and bougainvillea.

Two priests led seventeen-year-old Sanjay Gandhi to the pyre. The boy folded his grandfather's hands across his chest. He anointed him with holy water, and stepped back for a moment. Then, his hands trembling, the boy touched a torch to the wooden pyre. Flames shot upward.

"He is free of earthly bondage," the priests chanted.

"May he be immortal," the crowd responded.

Nehru wrote his own epitaph, describing himself as ". . . a man who with all his mind and heart loved the Indian people. And they in turn were indulgent to him and gave him of their love most abundantly and extravagantly."

India's problems remain far from solved. The nation's internal affairs, its economy, its standard of living are still urgent problems. The Indian dispute with Pakistan over Kashmir is still unsolved. Adding to all these worries, Chinese Red forces are still massed on India's borders, although Red China did call a cease-fire just at a time when the world felt that an all-out war was about to begin.

Nehru's position in world history will become clarified only with the passage of time. But in India, he will forever be enshrined next to the great leader, Mahatma Gandhi. As Gandhi has been called the "soul of India," Nehru has been proclaimed India's mind and her will toward betterment.

KWAME NKRUMAH

ALONG A TWISTING TRAIL through the African jungle a small boy rode astride his mother's back, his thin legs gripped firmly about her waist. The mother was walking the fifty miles from the boy's birthplace, Nkroful, to the village of Half Assini to join the boy's father and the rest of their family.

Forty-five years after that trip through the steaming jungle, this boy, grown to manhood, was to become the first black African leader of the first black African country to attain independence in this century.

He is Kwame Nkrumah. The country is Ghana, on the west coast of Africa just above the equator.

Nkrumah was barely three years old when he rode on his mother's back on the first leg of his long and hungry journey to the presidency of a new African nation. At that time Ghana was called the Gold Coast and it was a colony of Great Britain.

Ghana's independence was proclaimed on March 6, 1957, a date that has become a milestone in the history of Africa. Self-government for this small country of five million black Africans touched off a chain reaction among remaining dependent colonies on the Dark Continent. Within five years, flags of independence were flying over a dozen more new African nations.

Nkrumah became a symbol of the new Africa. He was inspiring proof that Africans were capable of self-government. His actions and leadership demonstrated to the world that Africans could govern themselves without the control or direction of European countries. Of most importance to other Africans, here was a man born in a primitive, jungle village who climbed to heights never before reached by a black African.

The climb was a difficult one for Nkrumah. In addition to the usual obstacles which strew the path of a poor young man striving for an education and success in life, Nkrumah was a black man in a world dominated by the white man.

Kwame Nkrumah (pronounced En-KROOM-ah) lived in the coastal village of Half Assini until he was eighteen years old. The exact year of his birth is uncertain; no records of births, marriages, or deaths were kept in Nkroful at the time he was born. His mother, Nyanibah, set the year as 1912. The priest who baptized him into the Roman Catholic Church recorded the birth date as September 21, 1909. The month September is more certain. That is the month of a national festival in Ghana. The day of the week is definite—Saturday. Most children in Ghana are named for the day of the week on which they are born, and Kwame is an African name for Saturday.

Kwame's father was a goldsmith. He melted down nuggets in clay molds, then beat out the softened gold into crude jewelry to be sold in larger towns and cities. His father had several wives, and all his wives and their children lived in the same mud-walled house. At no time were there fewer than fourteen wives and children in the house. Kwame was the youngest of his half-brothers and sisters. His mother was a market woman or trader. The wives took turns doing the cooking and caring for the children. When not occupied with these chores, a wife traveled from village to village with a large tray on her head, in which she carried the products she had to sell—fish, vegetables, fruit, or products made by her husband. Often Kwame went on these trips with his mother, walking beside her or riding on her back, bound tightly to her by a large fold in her dress. At night on these trips they slept outdoors beside a fire his mother would kindle.

It was this primitive background and mode of living that produced Kwame Nkrumah, Africa's first black leader.

Nkrumah went to school in a one-room elementary school in Half Assini for eight years. He then became a pupil-teacher. He was only about seventeen at the time, and so small that he had to stand on a box to write on the blackboard.

A turning point came in Nkrumah's life in 1926 when the principal of the Government Training College in Accra, the capital of the country, visited the school where Nkrumah was teaching. He was impressed with the young man's work and recommended that he go to college to train as a teacher.

After a year in the training college in Accra, Nkrumah transferred to the newly opened Prince of Wales College at Achimota, a few miles inland from Accra. He graduated from this college in 1930 and spent the next five years in various teaching jobs. He was the first black African to teach in a training school for Catholic priests, a school newly opened by the Jesuit Order at Amissano. Until then, Africans wanting to enter the priesthood had been sent overseas to be trained.

Baptized a Catholic, his early education supervised by Catholics, and himself a teacher in a Catholic school, Nkrumah for a short time considered entering the priesthood. His interest in politics, however, first kindled when teaching in Axim, was further fired when he attended a teachers' conference in Accra. There he heard Dr. Nnamdi Azikiwe, a Nigerian, make a fiery speech for African nationalism and lash out against British rule in African colonies. Dr. Azikiwe, who later became the first prime minister of Eastern Nigeria, exerted a strong influence on young Nkrumah. He had been educated in America, and Nkrumah was so impressed by the Nigerian that he was determined to go to America.

Nkrumah abandoned all thoughts of becoming a priest. As to his religious beliefs, he describes himself as a nondenominational Christian. "As I grew older," he wrote in his autobiography, "the strict discipline of Roman Catholicism stifled me. It was not that I became any less religious but rather that I sought freedom in the worship of and communion with God, for my God is a very personal God and can only be reached direct. I do not find the need of, in fact I resent, the intervention of a third party in such a personal matter."

During his teaching years, Nkrumah saved every penny he could for his passage to the United States. With these small savings, supplemented by a loan from a relative, he sailed for Liverpool, England, where he would have to obtain a visa to go to the United States. He made a trip to London while waiting, and there he saw a newspaper headline that stunned him: MUSSO-LINI INVADES ETHIOPIA.

"At that moment," Nkrumah wrote, "it was almost as if the whole of London had suddenly declared war on me personally. I could do nothing but glare at each impassive face wondering if those people could possibly realize the wickedness of colonialism, and praying that the day might come when I could play my part in bringing about the downfall of such a system. My nationalism surged to the fore; I was ready and willing to go through hell itself, if need be, in order to achieve my object."

Nkrumah arrived in the United States in the fall of 1935. He entered Lincoln University, a Negro college for men, in Pennsylvania. On his application for admission, he had written two lines from Tennyson's poem, "In Memoriam," which he called his spur and inspiration. They are:

> So many worlds, so much to do
> So little done, such things to be.

These words describe the impatient drive that has been a part of Nkrumah all his adult life. So little has been done, he feels, and there is so much to do in so little time if things in Africa are to be as he wants them.

Nkrumah graduated from Lincoln in 1939 and spent six more years in the United States. He spent this time in further study, working at any kind of a job to feed and clothe himself. He earned a master's degree in education and philosophy from the University of Pennsylvania and was working toward a doctorate in philosophy when he decided to return to Africa.

Of his ten years in the United States, Nkrumah wrote, "Those years in America and England were years of sorrow and loneliness, poverty and hard work. But I have never regretted them because the background that they provided has helped me to formulate my philosophy of life and politics."

They had been hard years. At times Nkrumah slept on park benches and rode the subway all night when he had no money for room rent. He worked summers on boats running between Philadelphia and Mexico, doing menial jobs. There was never enough money, and after he developed pneumonia while working in a shipyard outside Philadelphia, he decided, on recovering, that he would return to Africa.

As the ship carrying him to England sailed out of New York Harbor, Nkrumah looked at the Statue of Liberty. He wrote of this moment: "You have opened my eyes to the true meaning of liberty. I shall never rest until I have carried your message to Africa." In the years to come, however, Nkrumah closed his eyes to many of the liberties represented by the statue in New York's harbor.

Yet two more years were to pass before Nkrumah set foot once more on his native land. These years were spent in London, where he became active with other Africans in discussions and plans for the eventual freedom of African colonies from British and French rule.

He could think of nothing, speak of nothing but freedom for his country, and he was in a tremendous hurry
to achieve this goal.

During Nkrumah's second year in London, a movement toward independence was launched in Ghana. The
United Gold Coast Convention had been organized,
with its aim "to ensure that by all legitimate and consti-
tutional means the direction and control of government
should pass into the hands of the people and their chiefs
in the shortest possible time." The head of the UGCC,
Dr. J. B. Danquah, invited Nkrumah to return to Ghana
and become secretary of the organization. Nkrumah's
activities in London, his intense and urgent desire for
self-government, were well known in Ghana.

This purpose and Nkrumah's activities were even better known in London. Before he was permitted to leave
England, Nkrumah was questioned at length by British
authorities, and his passport was taken from him. The
British were concerned, and rightly so, as to what might
happen to their "model colony," as the Gold Coast was
known, with the return of Nkrumah. After several days
of questioning, Nkrumah's passport was returned to him
and he was permitted to sail for his homeland.

Back in Ghana, Nkrumah traveled through his country as secretary for the UGCC. He was an eloquent
speaker and a skilled organizer. More and more he came
into disagreement with the leaders of the UGCC. Their
announced course toward independence was too slow
for the fiery Nkrumah. He was for immediate self-
government. Nkrumah broke with the UGCC and
formed his own Convention People's Party, and his call
for "self-government NOW" became the battle cry of
the new party.

Nkrumah's campaign for immediate freedom brought

most of the UGCC members to his own party. Calling for "Positive Action" against the British government, Nkrumah ordered an illegal general strike and was sentenced to jail for two years. Ghana held its first general election in 1951 while Nkrumah was still in jail. His Convention People's Party scored such a decisive victory over the UGCC party that Nkrumah was released from jail to head the new government as its prime minister.

Nkrumah's popularity and the power of his Convention People's Party grew. The cry for "self-government NOW" became more insistent. In 1956, Great Britain agreed that if an election showed a clear-cut majority in favor of independence, England would release its hold on the Gold Coast on March 6, 1957. The election was held, and the vote was overwhelmingly for independence. The long struggle was over. The Gold Coast, Great Britain's "model colony," became Ghana, the first new black African country to attain independence in the 20th century. In 1960, Ghana cut its last ties from Great Britain when it voted to become a republic. Nkrumah became president of the republic, the head of state in name as well as in authority.

Nkrumah is an ambitious man and close observers of his career have seen many changes in the Ghananian leader since his rise to power. He has become the absolute ruler of his country. His hand-picked parliament passed a law in 1958 under which anyone speaking out against his government can be imprisoned for five years without trial. He has destroyed the opposition party by this law. Scores of its leaders and others opposing him have been jailed or exiled.

In addition to becoming ruler of Ghana, Nkrumah's

dream has long been to become the head of a United States of Africa. He has stated publicly many times, "I'm the leader of Ghana and since Ghana was the first independent African state, I am the leader of Africa."

Today there seems to be little possibility that Nkrumah will ever ride the crest of the upsurging continent of Africa. Other, much larger, African countries have achieved their independence, and their leaders do not look upon Nkrumah as the savior of Africa, as he has proclaimed himself.

In Ghana, though, Nkrumah is the supreme ruler. He is called by his own command *Osagyefo*, meaning "victorious leader." He has other titles as well. Among them are:

> *Ahuna Bo Birim*—"He whose presence electrifies."
> *Atenka*—"He whose fame is dreaded far and wide."
> *Bre Nsem Ase*—"He who is able to handle unmanageable events."
> *Oyeadieyie*—"Renewer of all things."

In Accra, the capital of Ghana, a newspaper headline proclaimed "Nkrumah is Ghana." There are huge bronze statues of Nkrumah in every city in Ghana. In Accra alone, there is a Kwame Nkrumah Railway Station, Kwame Nkrumah Circle, Kwame Nkrumah Avenue, Kwame Nkrumah Road, Kwame Nkrumah Leadership Training School, and a Kwame Nkrumah Cooperative. His head is etched on Ghananian coins and his picture appears on postage stamps.

Although Nkrumah states that he is a neutral, and

non-Communist, he is believed in recent years to be leaning more to the Soviet bloc than toward the United States and the Western bloc of nations. He has accepted financial aid from both blocs. He recently accused the Peace Corps, which has many members working in Ghana, of being agents for the United States Central Intelligence Agency.

The controlled press of Ghana is anti-Western; it subscribes to Tass, the Soviet news service, and to the New China News Agency, but to none of the Western news services.

Nkrumah is still strongly influenced by his education in the United States, although he seems to have forgotten the inspiration the Statue of Liberty gave him when he sailed out of New York Harbor in 1945.

Nkrumah has stated many times that he is a Christian. Still, he hangs on to many ancient African superstitions. He carries a cane, not to support himself, but to drive off evil spirits. To the armrests of his office chair there are attached several small leather bags containing strange objects to ward off evil spirits. When he was released from prison, he stepped seven times in the blood of a sheep to cleanse him from "the contamination of prison."

Nkrumah was married in 1957 to a Moslem from Egypt, a woman he had never seen, who was discovered by his representative in Cairo.

The Ghananian leader is a hard worker. He spends eighteen hours a day at his desk. He neither smokes nor drinks and has no form of recreation.

Although there seems to be little likelihood that he will ever become the black George Washington of a United States of Africa, Nkrumah remains a man of considerable influence through the continent. He is one of the most experienced of all the new African leaders. His position in his own country is still strong despite growing opposition, and he is still beloved by the majority of his people. It is believed that he will rule Ghana until his death.

No matter which way Kwame Nkrumah goes, to the east toward Russia, or the west toward the United States, and despite his dictatorship type rule, he will go down in history as the first black African leader of this century's first black African independent country. And where Nkrumah and Ghana led, other African nations have followed.

U THANT

ONE OF THE MOST difficult and thankless jobs in the world today is that of secretary-general of the United Nations. World forces—great powers and small ones—pull from all sides at the man holding this job. No matter how hard the pull, he must strive to keep to the middle of the road if the United Nations is to remain an effective, impartial organization in its work toward its ultimate goal—world peace.

The third man to hold this important and demanding position is U Thant, a quiet, soft-spoken gentleman from Burma. He was elected by the United Nations General Assembly on November 30, 1962, to serve a four-year term expiring November 3, 1966. The two men who preceded him as secretary-general were Trygve Lie of Norway, and Dag Hammarskjöld of Sweden.

U Thant (pronounced Oo Thawnt) was born at
Pantanaw, near Rangoon, Burma on January 22, 1909.
The "U" of his name is a term of respect, and is roughly
translated as the English "Mr." Thant is his only name;
he has no first or middle name. Thant, in English, means
"clean" or "pure."

The election of U Thant came after a year of sharp
controversy between the United States and Soviet Russia.
After the death of Dag Hammarskjöld in a plane crash
in Africa on September 18, 1961, Russia demanded that
the single or one-man secretaryship be replaced by a
troika, or three-man secretariat. Soviet Premier Nikita
Khrushchev declared that the machinery of the United
Nations had "grown rusty." The United Nations, he
said, should be completely reorganized, particularly the
top office.

The troika proposed by Russia would be composed of
one representative from the Communist bloc of nations,
one Westerner, and one representative of the neutral nations. The three would have to be in complete agreement
on any proposed action of the United Nations. A single
veto could kill the action. The United States flatly rejected Russia's proposal. Led by Adlai Stevenson, United
States Ambassador to the United Nations, the United
States insisted upon a single secretary-general, unfet-
tered by the veto, as set forth in the United Nations
charter.

Russia finally gave up on the troika, but then insisted
that the secretary-general have several assistant secre-
taries-general, any of whom could wield veto power
over their chief. Again, it was Ambassador Stevenson
who patiently but firmly carried negotiations with the
Soviet. At long last Russia retreated from this stand, too.

U Thant, as secretary-general, does have several assistants to advise him on important matters, but he is not bound to follow their advice nor do they have veto power over him.

While at college in Rangoon, U Thant met Thakin Nu, better known today as U Nu, former premier of Burma. This was the beginning of a long personal and political friendship between the two.

U Thant attended University College for only two years. The death of his father in 1928 forced him to conclude his formal education. He returned to Pantanaw, where he was appointed a senior master at his old high school, teaching English and modern history. Thakin had become headmaster of the school. U Thant's competitive drive and urge for further honors won him first place in the All-Burma Translation Competition sponsored by the Burma Education Extension Association. He was twenty years old at the time. Two years later he became headmaster of the Pantanaw High School when Thakin Nu left to study law at the University of Rangoon.

During World War II, Burma was overrun and occupied by the Japanese army. During these years, U Thant was secretary of a committee to reorganize Burma's educational system.

In the years preceding World War II, and immediately following, U Thant was active in the Burmese movement for independence, led by General U Aung San. Thant and Thakin Nu wrote many articles for newspapers and magazines criticizing colonialism. Burma at this time was still a British province. The pace of the movement for independence was stepped up with the return of the British to Burma in June of 1947, and the

Burmese assembly voted for complete independence. U Thant gave up his position as headmaster at the Pantanaw High School in 1947 to become press director for the interim government. On January 4, 1948, the Anglo-Burmese treaty establishing the Union of Burma went into effect. Four months later, in April, Burma became the fifty-eighth member of the United Nations.

U Thant held many governmental posts in the newly created republic. In turn, he was director of broadcasting, secretary in the Ministry of Information, secretary for projects for Prime Minister U Nu, and executive secretary of the Economic and Social Board. He was a close adviser to U Nu and accompanied him on many foreign missions.

In 1952, U Thant first saw the United Nations in action, when he was a member of the Burmese delegation to the seventh session of the General Assembly in New York. Five years later, in 1957, he was named Burma's permanent representative to the United Nations.

Although U Thant had been active in the United Nations for several years, he was still a somewhat obscure person when his name was first mentioned as a candidate for secretary-general to succeed Dag Hammarskjöld. It was generally agreed that the new secretary-general should come from one of the nations of Asia or Africa which were not committed to either the Communist Bloc of nations or to the Western Bloc.

The candidacy of U Thant was put forth by Dr. G. P. Malalasekera of Ceylon with the singing words: "In an age when strength is often equated with the booming voice and the bouncing fist, U Thant displays the strength of quiet dignity." The General Assembly elected him by the unanimous vote of 103 to 0.

U Thant described his attitude toward the important position in this way: "Whoever occupies the office of secretary-general must be impartial but not necessarily neutral. Countries can be neutral, but it is very difficult for an individual to be neutral on the burning questions of the day."

In his acceptance speech, U Thant pointed out the policy of nonalignment and friendship his own country had followed since it had become a republic. He stated that his intention was to "continue to maintain this attitude of objectivity and to pursue the ideal of universal friendship."

President Kennedy hailed U Thant's election as "a splendid achievement in which the whole world can rejoice."

There was no comment from the Soviet Union.

Since taking office, U Thant has rigidly maintained his position of independence in relation to both Communist and Western power blocs. Although he has stated that it is difficult for an individual to remain neutral, he is not in favor of a neutralist bloc of nations within the United Nations. He has rejected such proposals, saying the result would be "further splitting of an already divided world."

U Thant has criticized the actions and positions of both the United States and Soviet Russia. He believes that Communism, "however much we may detest it," is not the real enemy. The real enemy, he feels, is poverty, and the world stands divided today between the rich countries and the poor countries. He feels that the race between Russia and the United States to be first to put a man on the moon is "wantonly costly" in terms of money and in the resulting impact such a feat will have on the hungry peoples of the world. "No sensible person," he states "can believe that an American on the moon will make all hungry nations come flocking to the American flag."

The secretary-general has demonstrated his impartiality. He sharply criticized Russia for its suppression of the revolt in Hungary and was equally critical of the United States' role in the invasion of Cuba.

Disarmament has long been of primary concern to U Thant. Russia again felt his criticism when, in 1961, it resumed the unilateral testing of nuclear weapons. As for Communist China, he deplored its use of force in its dispute with Nationalist China over control of the off-shore islands of Matsu and Quemoy. The United States, he feels, was responsible in part for this crisis, because of its continued refusal to recognize the People's Republic of China.

U Thant demonstrated his capability for forceful action shortly after taking office. The Belgian Congo had become an independent nation in June of 1960, after seventy-five years as a Belgian possession. Immediately, chaos set in. Provinces seceded. Tribes fought tribes. Riots developed into bitter battles. It appeared that the Republic of the Congo would dissolve from internal struggles before it had even a start as an independent nation. Swift action by the United Nations followed an appeal for aid from the Congo. The province of Katanga, which had seceded, gave the most trouble. A "police force" made up of troops from eighteen nations moved in, and the United Nations ordered the immediate removal of mercenaries and foreign soldiers hired by Katanga. Several battles followed with casualties on both sides. Katanga finally yielded under United Nations pressure, and peace and unity were restored to the new republic.

In a large measure, U Thant is responsible for saving the United Nations from bankruptcy. At his suggestion the organization voted to issue $200,000,000 in twenty-five-year bonds, and these saved it from financial collapse.

U Thant's personal politics are those of democratic socialism. In Burma he belongs to a political party based on democratic principles and opposed to Communism.

In his private life, U Thant acts with the same restrained reasonableness he demonstrates in his official capacity. He is married to the daughter of a prominent Burmese lawyer. His only son, Tin Maung, was killed in a bus accident in 1962, but he has one daughter, Aye Aye, the wife of Tyn Myintu. She attended Hunter College in New York City.

U Thant is a neat five foot seven. He has a smooth, round face and iron-gray hair. He dresses in expensive, well-tailored Western suits for public appearances. At home in his New York City apartment, he relaxes and dons a native Burmese robe called a *longyi* or kilt. An author of several books himself, U Thant is an avid reader and belongs to six book clubs. Writing or reading, he chain-smokes expensive cigars.

As to the future of the United Nations, U Thant says: "Soon we shall see happier signs in the world. After all, no state has permanent friends or permanent enemies; only permanent interests."

INDEX